AUSTINTACIOUS

The Austintacious Quartet
Ostentatious but gracious

19th and University ·· BOOK I
Rebel Yell ·· BOOK II
Maya Karma ·· BOOK III
Austintacious ·· BOOK IV

BOOK IV

AUSTINTACIOUS
Crowded House

Fall Semester 1968

By
l.k. siga & BARBARA LIGHT LACY

Rising Times Books
A Division of Golightly Publishing

Austintacious:
Crowded house, Fall semester 1968

Copyright ©2018 Rising Times Books

ISBN 978-0-9966544-4-9 (paperback)
ISBN 978-0-9966544-5-6 (eBook)

Published in the United States by Rising Times Books,
A division of Golightly Publishing

P O Bos 181533
Dallas, Texas 75218-1533

Visit our website at www.risingtimesbooks.com

Cover Design: l.k. siga and Gary Oliver

Cover Graphics: Kerri Esten, Graphic Expressions

All rights reserved. No portion of this book may be reproduced, stored in a retrieval system, or transmitted in any other form or by any means—electronic, mechanical, photocopy, recording, scanning or other—except for brief quotations in critical reviews or articles without the written permission of the Publisher.

*For Fred (for inspiration),
GO, SJR, Bianca (for coverage) and Lonn Taylor*

At first light they left Rancho Quien Sabe in the Tajmobile and headed for Big Bend National Park. At Panther Junction they turned north and followed Highway 385 for the 69 miles to Marathon. There they turned east onto the Old El Paso-San Antonio route now called Highway 90. West of Sanderson they crossed the Great Comanche War Trail that went from Boquillas down on the Rio Grande up to Fort Stockton and Midland. At Dryden they took Highway 349 for the 59 miles north to Sheffield where they crossed Interstate 10 and went north a hundred miles through Iraan and Rankin to Midland's intersection with Interstate 20. The Tajmobile would be heading east the rest of the way.

Forward, beyond the Tajmobile's companionway, Johnny Cash's "Folsom Prison Blues" could be heard. "That's the live version Cash recorded in January of 1968 at Folsom Prison," Ben Jack Gage said to Tres. The only grandfather Tres had ever known was strumming his Mexican six string guitar while leaning James Dean style against the wall between a drawing of Don Quixote and a poster of the 1967 Be In held in San Francisco's Golden Gate Park. On the floor beside Jack was Charles Dickens' A Tale of Two Cities. As usual, Jack wore Levis and a T-shirt, the front of today's T-shirt saying **"That's weather...Sports is next."**

"Where are we now?" Jen said from her bentwood rocker..

"We're almost to Big Spring, hon," Jack said. "They got a federal prison there too."

i

chapter one

Again to Austin then.

After a week at sea, Michael A. was riding shotgun in a refrigerated truck hauling a ton of marijuana concealed beneath two tons of frozen redfish. The truck had come from the tiny port of Kemah and was en route to the Blackfeet Nation in Montana. The truck was in Austin now, stopping at Interstate 35's exit for 19th Street and Walks In Blue Green was saying:

"Mission accomplished, Michael A. You gave maximum effort. Your dad would've been proud."

"Caca pasa, chachalaca. Onward through the fog," said Michael A. Then he adjusted his rose colored glasses and got out of the truck for the five-block walk through Austin's prickly September heat, his sockless, white Converse tennies discombobulated, his cutoffs grungy, his T-shirt saying *Quiet Please, One At A Time* a tattered rag. After trudging past Sabine, Red River, San Jacinto, Speedway and Wichita to 19th and University, he came upon a horde of hippies walking south. They were decked out in their finest hippie chic and one of them gave him a handbill. On the handbill and beneath a Jim Franklin armadillo was printed the following:

The Vulcan Gas Company presents New Atlantis and The Lavender Hill Express at Wooldridge Park, September 29, 1968.

When Michael A. arrived at the bottom of 200 West 19th's twelve steps, he was being greeted by Hannah the cat when he saw his household's newest member sitting in a purple butterfly chair on the front porch. Michael A. was too slaphappy to recall her name but he did ogle her: long dark hair, luscious breasts in yellow tank top, her humma-humma hips in white short-shorts. Uncrossing her fine long legs, she said:

"Like what you see?"

"Yes'm. You look awful good."

"And you look like something the cat dragged in." Then she winked and said, "But I think it's groovy that you're growing your hair long."

Michael A. went up the porch steps, plopped down in the other purple butterfly chair and said, "Are ya settled in yet?"

"Yep, Ryder'n Jack fixed me up out back. Did you come in the reefer truck?"

"'Re*fri*gerated' truck, please." Then he stretched his arms, took a long deep breath and said, "I've had no sleep since the equinox and, oh, what a long strange passage it was."

"But now our sailor home is home from the sea."

"Some sailor—I was a landlubber without sea legs on a seven-day sail with four-hour watches an' only eight hours off. With the trade wind aft we were on a broad reach that heeled us over an' fallin' off four to six-foot swells. I spent the first day hanging over the lifeline callin' Ralph."

"Who's Ralph?"

"Ralph Barf. As in seasick, puke city—*rrraaalph!*"

"Yech."

"Check. An' with no Nacho to captain us me'n Scuba'n Chel didn't use our imagination, didn't advise ourselves an' lots of times we couldn't even see where we were going. Three days out a squall pooped us an' we lost the engine. Then for a whole day we pitched an' rolled through a storm. Finally we get to the continental shelf an' dead ahead is a line of tankers anchored stem to stern awaiting entry to the Houston Ship Channel. We durn near had our forty-foot-tall main mast sheared off tryin' to get through those tankers' stretched-out anchor chains. Then just before dawn on the last day we come to Bolivar Roads, a strip of water bordered north'n south by jettys'n east'n west by Galveston Island an' Bolivar Peninsula. We almost ran aground the south jetty 'cause we're lookin' for a lighthouse that turned out to be a little 'ol bitty signal light. By dawn we're in Bolivar Roads which is less than a mile wide. Dawn is rush hour so ship traffic is comin' out of Galveston Bay, the Houston Ship Channel an' the Inter Coastal Canal. Meanwhile we're tryin' to sneak unseen past the customs house by usin' a big ol' freighter as a blind when a tug boat captain yells at us through his bull horn, "You're either nuts or you gotta lotta nuts to be out here this time of day in a *dad*blamed sailboat!" Here Michael A. sighed before saying, "An' when I stepped off the *Zak Be* in Kemah twenty miles later, I fell to my knees—not in gratitude but 'cause I didn't have my land legs."

"Well, you made it an' all's well that ends well," she said. Then she stood up to wave at a woman on the corner and say, "Be right there, Mrs. Smalley."

"You going somewhere with the neighbor lady?"

"Yep, our first love-in. I can't wait to hear Que Tal."

"Whoa! My band has a gig today?"

"Yep, Que Tal's the warmup band. Walks In Blue Green didn't tell you?"

"I honestly don't know. He might have told me, but I'm so tired I can't even recall your name."

"Ya big silly," she said then winked again and turned to strike the pose that made Betty Grable famous as a pin-up girl in World War II: grinning at him over her left shoulder, hands on her hips, her gorgeous and sumptuous buns straining within her white short-shorts. This pose brought Michael A. fully awake and he was grinning like a banshee when he said to her:

"Well, hellooo, Two Moons."

. . .

They walked to Wooldridge Park via Lavaca Street because Mrs. Smalley said she wanted to see La Vaca Lana.

"It used to be a furniture store," she said.

"Yep," said Michael A. "It was where my folks bought me my first bed. That was in 1954 when Dad was stationed at Camp Mabry."

Two Moons said, "I know that 'vaca' means 'cow' in Spanish, but what's 'lana' mean?"

"It's Texian slang for 'cash money'," said Mrs. Smalley.

"Texian?"

"That's what Texans were first called. My ancestors were Texians. In the 1830s they came to Texas from Yucatan with Lorenzo de Zavala. He was was first provisional vice president of the Republic of Texas. He also designed the republic's first flag."

"The one we got now?" said Michael A.

"Nope, it had a blue field with a star in the center," said Mrs. Smalley. "Now tell me about this La Vaca Lana enterprise."

"La Vaca Lana is a registered and licensed importer of Yucatecan honey, hammocks and chanclas."

"Wonderful," said Mrs. Smalley. "I can't get that stuff since my Yucatecan cousin passed on."

Michael A. said, "La Vaca Lana also has food purveyors. There's veggie dishes an' earth food at Oedibles. Mayapan is a tortilla factory an' bakery. Viva Zapatas has chanclas and Piegan Indian moccasins, also Piegan war shirts, dance sticks, flutes, drums, whistles, rattles, walking sticks, tomahawk pipes, beaded medicine bags. Hoochie Mamas has hippie clothes, generic T-shirts plus bumper stickers an' head shop stuff. And then there's Reruns which is a used book an' record store." After a pensive pause, Michael A. said:

"I wonder what ever happened to that bed my folks bought here."

chapter two

They walked down to 10th Street to Wooldridge Park's bandstand. There, while Que Tal tuned their instruments and did microphone checks Two Moons got a history lesson.

"Wooldridge Park," Bicycle Annie said, "is one of four original public squares appointed in the 1839 municipal plan for Austin by Edwin Waller. It was vacant for 70 years. In 1909 Mayor A.P. Wooldridge put in the gazebo-like bandstand. The park is one city block, a natural basin that forms an amphitheater for the bandstand in the center."

After the love in, Michael A. and Two Moons walked to Cambridge Tower at 1801 Lavaca. Here they took the elevator 181 feet above the earth to the roof deck.

"Wow," said Two Moons, "there's the UT Tower. Over there's our house. The Capitol building is right there and you can look all the way down Congress Avenue to its bridge over the river."

"That part of the river is called Town Lake," said Michael A. "Beside the Congress Avenue Bridge is the Sheraton Crest Inn at 111 First Street. It was built in 1965 on the site of Austin's first hotel, the Colorado house. Town Lake itself was once part of the Chisholm Trail and was enhanced in 1960 when the Longhorn Dam was built to create a chilling station for the Holly Street Power Plant."

Two Moons then pointed at the hills to the west and said, "Hey, look, it's purplish over there."

"Yep," Michael A. said. "Some say that's why the writer O. Henry called Austin 'the city of the violet crown.'"

"And what's that way down there?" Pointing at a bunch of campfires on Town Lake's north shore.

"A hobo camp. The street people call it 'the K.O.A.'"

"Whoa!" Two Moons said, now pointing at the Congress Avenue Bridge. "What's that flying out from under the Congress Avenue Bridge?"

"Bats," Michael A. said. "This is cave country an' when Town Lake was built it covered up the bats' caves so they've relocated to beneath the bridge."

"Ouuu, that means bat ghosts. This sweet little Piegan girl don't like ghosts."

Hearing that, Michael A. decided not to tell her the local legend about an Indian burial ground.

Or about Mona.

. . .

Because Michael A. wanted to see what Two Moons had meant by "Ryder'n Jack fixed me up out back", they walked to the driveway of 200 West 19th where, beyond Jack's 1956 Ford pickup and Cool Breeze's 1956 pink Cadillac, was Two Moons' eighteen-foot-high tipi. As Michael A. approached its buffalo hide shell painted with the ancient symbol known as "the Sacred 'G'," three goats tethered in front of the tipi began to bleat.

Using his favorite Maya greeting, Michael A. said "Bis be" to the goats and they shut up. Then he tapped on the horseshoe nailed to the lodge pole above the flap that was the tipi's door and said, "I bet Jack put this horseshoe here."

Two Moons said, "Jack said it's a Texas tradition. I'm supposed to keep the legs pointed up so the luck won't run out."

"Well, you just got lucky, lady," Michael A. said. The he pulled open the tipi's flap and with a lascivious grin on his face said, "Wanta make whoopee?"

"Nope"—making a face—"it's a sweat lodge in there."

"Living in Austin means handling the heat, Two Moons, especially in September." Next he gestured toward the tipi and said, "C'mon, we done it before."

"Shih tah hay, Michael A. If this sweet little Piegan girl's gonna be a lawyer for the Blackfeet Nation's Piegan tribe, she's got no time for love."

"What's love got to do with it? I make you feel good, you do the same for me." But seeing he was getting nowhere, he let go of the tipi's flap and said, "How come ya brought the goats?"

"Nachita, Nubia and Monita are my guard goats."

"Smart move. There are some rough hombres that prowl our alley. What do your goats eat?"

"Weeds. I hired them out to Mrs. Smalley to clean her yard."

"Mrs. Smalley's a cheapskate. She pays peanuts."

"Actually, she pays in peaches and pecans." Two Moons then reached inside her tipi and brought out Jen's two olive green Samsonite suitcases. Handing them to him, she said, "This is the payment for the Kemah mota."

"Cool," Michael A. said and took the Samsonites, went over to Cool Breeze's 1956 pink Cadillac, put them in the trunk. Next he said, "Let's celebrate by making the scene. Mouse an' the Traps are at the New Orleans Club. The Kings are at the Jade room. The One Knite at 801 Red River is a *grrreat* dive."

Two Moons grinned hopefully and said, "Are these places air-conditioned?"

"Nooo, but up on the roof we got a cool spot where you can stop your grinnin'n drop your linen."

"Cowabunga, but you're a Force of Nature, arencha?"

"Ya ain't seen nothin' yet, darlin'."

. . .

With Boo Boo the chick in her hair and Hannah in her lap Two Moons was stretched out next to Michael A. in his hamaca up in the Crow's Nest and saying:

"What's a chicken fried steak?"

"Tenderized cube steak breaded with seasoned flour that's pan fried'n served covered in cream gravy with french fries on the side. Hill's Steak House on South Congress has got the bestest."

This was when Boo Boo went "*Cheep!*" and Hannah went on guard, ears pricked, twitching her tail from side to side before leaping out of Two Moons' lap to scurry atop the red chimney.

"My instincts tell me this house is alive," said Two Moons.

"Please don't say that."

"Wait. What's that sound? Do I hear a bell ringing?"

"Best not ask for whom the bell tolls, sweet little Piegan girl."

chapter three

From the front porch Que Tal could hear Ma in the downstairs bedroom singing a Lebanese lullaby to put Baby Maya down for the night. Because dessert would be hand-cranked homemade ice cream made with Mrs. Smalley's peaches, Jack was in the bentwood rocker cranking the handle of a White Mountain ice cream maker that Ryder had found. Next to him in a purple butterfly chair Jen was saying:

"We were a wee eensy snitch rusty at the love-in."

"We were a train wreck," Michael A. said from the other purple butterfly chair. "I had no stage presence an' I was slow on the uptake."

Jack, cranking away on the ice cream maker, said, "The only good thing was that New Atlantis let us use their equipment."

"Yeah," Michael A. said, "it was nice not having to break our stuff down here then haul it out to the Fitty Six, load it then drive down to Wooldridge Park to find a parking place only to unload again and set up."

"Then have to repeat the whole rigamarole to get it back home," said Taj from his seat on the top porch step.

"We need to practice'n get back in the groove," said Natasha who was seated next to Taj.

"No question about it," Jack said, shaking his head. "But I think my guitar licks were also lame 'cause I'm a country boy who's a mite bashful about playin' in front of so many folks."

Natasha said, "Because of the crowd noise I couldn't hear what I was playing on my keyboard."

Taj said, "The connectivity of my rhythm was off because the drums were not placed in the manner to which I am accustomed."

Jen, putting salt on the ice around the canister, said, "That guitar string I broke flustered me so bad it took five minutes to change it."

"Did you guys ever look into us getting 801 Red River?" Michael A. said.

"Yep," Jack said. "It's not for sale, just for lease."

"And Xutan Partners doesn't lease," Natasha said.

"Leasing property is a circumsized idea financially," Jen said.

"But if we had 801 Red River, we could practice there an' not have to move our equipment," Michael A. said. "Also, if we were the house band we'd get used to playing in front of people. Besides, getting The One Knite ain't about making money. It's about us giving something back to the counterculture that's made us rich'uns. The One Knite would be a smaller, more intimate evolution of The Vulcan Gas Company. A hippie club that's open every night an' has affordable live music."

"I'm all for it, Cuz," Jack said, cranking the ice cream maker's handle harder.

"I too find the idea most appealing," Taj said.

Jen made a face and said, "A beer joint for longhairs?"

Natasha said, "Have you seen The One Knite? It's a dump."

"Nawww," Jack said, big smile on his face. "It's a dive is what it is. The One Knite Dive & Tavern." Then, seeing Jen wince at this, he cranked even harder and said, "I like dives."

Michael A. said, "C'mon, think of it. There won't be another dive in Austin like The One Knite Dive & Tavern."

"I like dives," Jack said again.

"Selling booze means drunks," Natasha said.

"And they bring cops," Jen said. "There'd be busts."

Jack pushed the ice cream maker over to Taj and said, "I say we owe it to ourselves to give it a shot."

"I agree," Taj said then grunted because it was tough cranking now.

Jen said, "We know nothing about the bar business."

"It's not like if it flops, we'd be wiped out," Jack said.

Taj stopped cranking and said, "The ice cream will be ready after dinner." Which was when Bicycle Annie yelled from the kitchen:

"*Spaghetti Squash Fritters a la Taj! Come and get it!*"

Jack stood up, picked up the White Mountain wooden bucket and said, "Just exactly what is a 'tavern' anyway?"

"Forget that," Natasha said, giving Michael A. a stern look. "Somebody tell me what a clean break is."

"Hey, look," Taj said, pointing at the underside of the White Mountain wooden bucket. "It says 'Made In 1868.'"

"And right here," Jen said, pointing below, "is carved 'Mona D. 1910.'"

. . .

After Michael A. had scarfed up Spaghetti Squash Fritters a la Taj, oh, how the mighty did fall: face first into his plate. Whereupon Jack calmed everyone with "He's done this before" then with Taj's help dragged the Fallen One to the faded red couch in the living room. There Jen cleaned his spaghetti-sullied face with his tattered and torn *QUIET PLEASE, ONE AT A TIME* T-shirt while Natasha took off his discombobulated Converse tennies.

"Even his godawful ugly toes are dead to the world," she said.

. . .

Jack was saying to Jen, "Wanta boot-scoot down at The Broken Spoke?"

"We can't. We have Baby Maya to take care of."

"Maybe Aunt Sofi will—"

"It's Sunday night so she's got church."

Jack and Jen were in their bedroom. Jen was on the water bed holding George Orwell's *Animal Farm* but mostly watching Jack try to braid his hair into a ponytail as he sat in her boudoir on the fruit crate used for a vanity stool. When Jack gave up braiding to rub his beard stubble, Jen said:

"I think you should grow a mustache like George Harrison's." Then she said with a grin, "Or a beard like that Fabulous Furry Freak Brother? The one with the ponytail?"

"Freewheelin' Franklin," Jack said, going into the bathroom.

Jen grinned some more and said "I bet your mustache'd look like that piddly little caterpillar James Dean had in *Giant*."

"He called it his 'pencil thin mustache,'" Jack said, starting to sharpen Granpa Gage's old straight razor on the leather strop hanging on the wall. But he abruptly set down the razor and said, "You know what, hon? I'm sick'n tired of using Granpa Gage's straight razor. It takes too durn long to strop it to a fine enough edge."

"Try one of my Lady Schicks," Jen said, teasing. "There's a brand new one on the bathtub."

"Nawww. They're for women."

"Skin is skin, you male chauvinist pig."

"But it's pink!"

"It' also plastic and therefore disposable."

"Whut it is," Jack said, some put-down in his voice, "is future landfill fodder. Not very environmentally friendly is the Throwaway Society."

As he struggled with the Lady Schick's packaging, Jen said, "Big John's House of Crap has an Ethan Allen boudoir. Do you think it'd be okay if we hit up the three lock box for the moolah to buy it?"

"Oh hell yeah. It's spending money, ain't it? And didn't you hear Michael A. say we're rich'uns?" Then, frustrated at his inability to open the package, he put set it aside and said, "I'm giving up shaving."

"So you're gonna do the Freewheelin' Franklin bit?"

"Nooo"—sounding peeved—"I'm just gonna be me."

. . .

"Where am I?" she said.

"Stuck here in the middle with me," Taj said as he finished hanging a dreamcatcher above the matrimonial hamaca given them by Nacho. He was nude but Natasha was not.

"I am a tree without roots," she said. "I am Eno Onmai."

"'I Am No One' spelled backwards," he said. Then he smiled his gentle smile at her and said, "Natasha, you *are* someone, someone very special to me."

"Someone who doesn't know who her parents are."

"You are Nacho's heiress. As Michael A. says, you're a 'richness.'"

"Why'd Nacho do that to a gal raised on goat's milk?"

"La maya work in mysterious ways. Do you recall our Maya names? You are Dawn Song and I am Bridge Beyond the Light."

"Everyman and Eno Onmai is more like it. Anyway I won't know the full extent of my inheritance until I go back to the island in December. Only the *Zak Be* and Hotel Tulan have been mentioned, which is problematic since revolutionaries eschew luxuries." Sounding wistful, she said, "I miss Cozumel and Akumal. I miss seeing the stars down there in Where The Sky Is Born and Place of the Turtle."

"Starlight comes from light emitted eons ago. It is the past arriving for us to see." Teasing her with a smile, he said, "We are but star flowers sown here by cosmic winds."

Again sounding wistful, she said, "Nacho said scuba diving made us transcendent beings. I miss tumbling an' freefalling head over heels into the depths of our Blue Planet's birth in that nutrient soup that is the sea."

"I would still be a mute if not for diving," he said.

"Diving did me plenty of justice too," she said.

"Speaking of the sea, today while watching Hannah lap up her bowl of milk my mind's eye magnified the little waves her tongue were making until I imagined that I was seeing the waves on Akumal Bay. My assumption is that my mind was alerting me to the beginnings of an idea."

Natasha grinned. "Was there ouu-spooky music too?"

"You *are* an anarchist, aren't you?" he said, grinning back.

She did not answer, just said, "Maybe it wasn't an alert your mind sent you but a notice like xutan. According to Marshall McCluhan, the music of our generation is a beacon telling the old culture what's starting to happen to it." Then she gave him that certain look and said, "Wanta do it?"

So they then got down to the physical pleasure of love. The unmitigated rapture of sensual joy. Once they had sated themselves of the physical aspect of this glorious desire, they relaxed in the afterglow, a pleasure they shared anew, same as when they had first lain together in his small bed beside the window, that window now wide open, both of them drenched in the sweet sweat of their lovemaking. Natasha's right cheek lay upon his chest hair and, as he ran his fingers through her hair, she said:

"Within each of us is an artist we do not yet know."

"And," Taj said, "when I say the word 'you' I speak of one hundred universes.'"

"A cyclical journey forever revolving forward like the Milky Way itself. Where you can see 'what it was' so you can live with 'what it is' then maybe see 'what it's gonna be.' A winding, up and down Road where it's not the years or the mileage as much as it's the take-offs and the landings."

"Our story is the Maya riddle 'What is a traveler on the Road of Life?'"

"'Time' is the answer and time is the tapestry within which we dwell. The place without a place in which we live and can never escape."

"We're all Maya in these rising times of future past."

"The center of this house shall never die."

"Does that mean you wanta do it again?"

"You bet."

. . .

Two Moons was asleep in her tipi when a bump in the night alerted her goats to a presence outside. But the presence dropped to the ground and rolled out of sight beneath Jack's pickup when Two Moons switched on her flashlight. Then, while belly-crawling to the Fitty Six's driver's side in order to get to his lair, the clumsiness of this presence pulled loose the brake line. And once safe in his lair, The Voice started in again, saying:

"Hear me, Evil. None may know your ugliness for not even daylight sees you nor does dust find you. Darkness is your only friend … so find a shadow to hide in."

chapter four

As John Lennon sang "Imagine," Tres was saying, "Was Nacho's passing the inspiration for that Que Tal lyric, 'A rich man dies, a newborn cries and on and on it goes'?"
Jack said, "Yep. Most of us in Que Tal figured losing Nacho was the clean break that would get us out of The Life."
"But opinions vary," Jen said.

. . .

Bicycle Annie parked the 1956 pink Cadillac in the shade of the majestic old live oak at 507 Baylor and said to Que Tal, "This is the Austin landmark known as Treaty Oak. This tree is five hundred years old and they say that Tejas Indian women drank a tea made from honey and its acorns as part of a ritual to keep their warriors safe. In the 1830s this spot had fourteen trees and became known as Council Oaks when Stephen F. Austin, leader of the Austin colony, negotiated a treaty with the Indians after a judge and two kids got killed. By 1927 only this one oak tree remained due to neglect and expansion."

Annie then vacated the vehicle so as to make herself scarce because inside the Caddy the vibe was volatile. And, sure enough, once Annie began to gather Treaty Oak acorns, Jen scooted over into the driver's seat then turned to Michael A. in the back seat between Taj and Jack and said:

"You're a big ol' fibber, Miguel Antonio Medina."

Michael A. shrugged and said, "Who among us is perfect?"

"You've become jaded 'cause you think it's cool," said Natasha from the front seat.

"I most certainly have *not* become jaded. Being jaded is highly overrated."

"Us havin' all this pot has got to end, Michael A.," Jen said.

"What pot?" he said. "All we got in our possession is that piddlin' puny amount in the Hotpoint's freezer."

"Cool the silver-tongued-devil bit, spitbird," Natasha said. "We agreed to make a clean break from The Life."

"And Nacho's passing was that clean break," Jen said.

"But what does our boy Michael A. do?" Natasha said. "He sails up from Cozumel with a new load."

Jen said, "You lied to us, Michael A., and that's a pretty cruddy thing for one hippie do to another."

"Nothin' cruddy about 240K more moolah in the three lock box," he said and showed his grin. Next he took off his rose colored glasses and said wearily, "Look, y'all, life is change an' life is compromise an' it's not like I actively sought the *Zak Be* pot. Nacho had already set up the smuggle an' when he passed, well, Chel an' Scuba needed me so I hadda be a standup guy."

Jack now spoke up, "Nacho never told Cuz nothin'. Same as when he painted my Fitty Six baby spit yellow or all those times he glued a plastic Jesus to its dashboard."

"Anyway, we got no problem," Michael A. said. "The load is in Montana at The Rez an' The Rez is a sovereign nation."

"You're not listening, Michael A.," Natasha said, "This illegal enterprise you've foisted on us has got to stop."

"Nothin' got *foisted* on you. I merely practiced hippie values as in 'share'n share alike' an' as a result we now not only got moolah out the wah-zoo, we own our house, Castle Hostel, La Vaca Lana an' other real estate plus stuff from Big John's, groceries, band equipment, generic T-shirts, motorcycles. I was just an errand boy for Smuggler Nacho an' Trafficker Tunoose."

Jack said, "He's sure 'nough right about Nacho. That old ringtail tooter was a smuggler before we were born. He flat out did not respect man-made borders."

Michael A. said, "And Uncle Tunoose has been trafficking in fad knockoffs for years. Slinkys, Hula Hoops, Frisbees, whatever was happenin.'"

"That was then, this is now," Jen said, "and pot's no fad. It can do *wayyy* more harm than the crabs infestation you sprung on us last spring. Jack and I are parents now and we don't want to go to jail or be labeled dope fiends."

Taj now spoke up, saying, "Cannabis is only illegal due to a smear campaign by Big Business in the 1930s to eliminate hemp as cotton's competition."

Jack said, "An' that film *Reefer Madness* was part of the smear. Granpa Gage told me all about it. He said that hemp's better than cotton for clothing an' that, unlike cotton, hemp is resistant to bugs. The rich and powerful people behind fertilizer and insecticide wanted it out of the way."

"An' like history," said Michael A., "laws are written by those in power."

Taj said, "Hemp is merely an herb, another of Mother Nature's wonders sown in her earth. It is not one of man's processed nightmares. Nor is it a hydrogen bomb."

"It's not as bad as booze," Michael A. said. "We are *not* Public Enema Number One. We are just the 'enemy who is us'. We're that part of the counterculture which profits off the underground economy. But, relax, there won't be any more smuggling in the *Zak Be* because its mota was grown on the future site of Cancun International Airport."

Taj said, "And let us not forget that more than marijuana was aboard the *Zak Be*. La Vaca Lana now has hamacas, chanclas and barrels of Yucatecan honey."

"How clever and original," Jen said, being facetious. "Who'd ever suspect La Vaca Lana as a front for an international dope ring?"

"'International dope ring' my cute patoot," Jack said. "Nacho wasn't a bad guy an' Uncle Tunoose ain't either. Both of 'em always had our best interests at heart."

Natasha said to Michael A., "Well, what's with that leather pouch full of diamonds Rosko gave you?"

"Rosko's a riddle. But those diamonds have staying power an' they can't be traced."

"They can't be explained either," Jen said.

"Nor can what's in the three lock box," Natasha said.

"Then leave us find a hidey-hole," said Michael A.

"Perhaps we should put Ryder on such a quest," said Taj. "That fellow is obviously looking for something at 200 W. 19th."

"Ryder's another riddle, no question about it," Michael A. said. "Be that as it may, I say we let La Vaca Lana an' Purple People Eater launder some of the cash an' the rest we stash in a hidey-hole."

Jen said to Natasha, "Actually, I'd like to use some of the money to pay off my parents' debts."

"An' don't forget about baby stuff," Jack said.

"And a bedroom set," Jen said.

"Winter's coming," Michael A. said, "so we should score some gas heaters for the house."

Natasha sighed and said, "I'd sorta like to donate to the Free Clinic and the Crusade Against the Evil Rich."

"And I wish to invest in a company in California," Taj said. "Also a recording studio and a radio station."

Jack said to Jen, "An' I told you on my birthday I wanta buy a farm up on the Caprock. Remember?"

"I do," Jen said. "And when will you accept the fact that the Fitty Six is a dinosaur?"

Jack said, "You're right, hon. The clock is ticking on my baby."

There now came a silence until Michael A. said, "So do we keep on keepin' on with The Life?"

"It does not appear that we want out," said Taj, "and thus our little chrysalis has come to yet another crossroads."

Michael A. said, "Hey, we're Que Tal. We're good for each other an' we work and play well together. If we're careful an' keep our cool, at the very least we get a leg up in this dog-eat-dog world, maybe even be set up for life, maybe even jolt The Establishment while we're at it. But it's gotta be all of us or none. One for all an' all for one. We don' want to be martyrs leavin' the battlefield laid out on our shields. We want to come out winners with our swords held high."

Natasha said, "What's Mrs. Medina say about it?"

"Ma's all for it."

There was another silence as Natasha and Jen exchanged whispers then Jen said to Michael A., "No more smuggling?"

"Cross my heart." Showing her a quiet smile the same way he believed Steve McQueen would. "We just got a few loose ends to take care of—Red Fred, Walks in Blue Green, Cacciatore'n Mugsy. The rest of you guys can be university students and"—putting his rose colored glasses back on'—"in my spare time I'll be a commercial-minded cartoonist content to be Que Tal's bass player."

"Bull," Natasha said. "You'll always be a silver-tongued devil."

"Mish posh," said Bicycle Annie now beside the Pink Caddy with her acorns. "Bourgeois capitalists is what all y'all is."

. . .

That night at band practice Que Tal worked up The Animals' version of "Oh Lord Please Don't Let Me Be Misunderstood." Michael A. was the one who sang it, of course.

. . .

Though the 19th and University kids called him "Mona," he called himself "What Goes Bump In The Night." And it was all Tunoose's fault. What Goes Bump In The Night had always minded the store at the 19th Street house. Sure he had boosted a hula hoop here, a frisbee there and, yeah, he had pawned some of the house's old-timey stuff, but What Goes Bump In The Night never figured on Tunoose giving him the boot. So he did a dirty deed then took a powder by moving into the 19th Street house's root cellar. He had been down there that day back in January, 1968, when Michael A. and Jack and Jen came to the front door and its old timey ringer broke off in Michael A.'s hand. As Mona he had had some fun with the kids, particularly with Michael A.—freaking him out by singing "I Know You Rider" to him being the most fun. And once or twice he had put the touch on the three lock box because a guy had to eat. And all through 1968 What Goes Bump In The Night had eavesdropped on the 19th Street kids. He had listened in on them while they were in the living room, the dining room, the kitchen, their bedrooms, even while they were in their hamacas up in the Crow's nest. He had listened to them making music down in the White Room, and in his opinion they weren't bad. But it was when What Goes Bump In The Night developed a derelict lust for the one who had robbed him of redemption that The Voice entered his life. Right now the Voice was saying to him:

"Natasha is a horrible girl so use her up. I like her 'Eno Onmai' bit but she's saying she can 'slip inside this house', so it's time she learned that *I* am the center of this house and *I* shall never die."

What Goes Bump In The Night wished The Voice would just shut up.

chapter five

With the exception of drop-out Michael A. the University's academic side of life had saddled every 19th Street kid with eight o'clock classes. At dawn, Monday, September 30, Jack and Jen and Baby Maya were asleep in their waterbed when Jack awoke, but not to the usual thump of the *Austin American* landing on the front porch. Instead, a ray of light had penetrated the dwindling fall foliage of Wiley and Beep Beep's favorite oak tree and invaded the bedroom. Once inside it reflected off the mirror in Jen's boudoir then crossed the room to sear into Jack's left eyelid. Instinct then made Jack scooch up in bed and rest his head against the wall. Fully awake now, he smiled at a stack of *Daily Texans* that were special to him and Michael A. because each had a screw-up coupon from the Scho Pro Lounge: $1 pitchers of beer without an expiration date. Tilting his head upwards, Jack smiled some more at the very first photograph of Maya Karma Gage. Jolinda Biggs had taken the photo yesterday when mother and child had arrived at Austin's Mueller Municipal Airport. Jack now looked down at his daughter asleep between him and Jen and thought:

You're not even two weeks old but you rule my world.

Jack looked at Jen and was glad that Boo Boo the chick had bonded with Taj and no longer slept in Jen's hair. This was when Jen winced then whimpered and a twitching of her foot drew Jack's attention to a reddish brown spider there. After dispatching it, he heard:

"Jaaack?"

"Yeah, hon?"

"I dreamed—"

"It's proper to say 'dreamt', Jen."

"Oh, piffle. Anyway, I was dreaming I was on a mountain and I fell off and hurt my ankle."

Jack swept away the dead spider and said, "You know what Nacho would say about your dream, don't you?"

"Yeah. 'Dreams are portals to the Spiritworld.'" Then Jen winced again and said, "My ankle hurts."

. . .

While the others in the house were away for their first day of classes and Ma and Baby Maya were on the front porch, a rested Michael A. was on the faded red couch in the living room catching up on last week's news in the *Austin American* and *American Statesman*.

The September 22 newspaper said that the United States Marines had invaded the Demilitarized Zone, that Soviet troops had pulled out of Czechoslovakia and that the University of Texas football team had battled to a 20-20 tie with the University of Houston.

On Monday, September 23, the Soviets recovered an unmanned spacecraft that had circled the moon and two more U.S. airliners were hijacked to Cuba. There was a photo of Danny the Red Cohn Bendit trying to crash a peace award ceremony. Zuider Zee at 5011 Burnet Road had all the shrimp you could eat for $2.75. There was a story on page 12 saying that the control of an unborn's sex was but five years away.

The September 24 paper quoted United Nations Secretary General U Thant as declaring that the majority of the General Assembly would support a resolution for the U.S. to stop bombing Vietnam, that the assets of San Antonio's Hemisfair top its liabilities, that the Austin city council okayed a $75.5 million budget and Davis Hardware had a full page ad advertising transistor pocket size radios for $3.95.

The September 25 headline story was that, according to top Republican Melvin Laird, the Johnson administration was planning its first troop slash of 90,000 men between now and June 30. Fowler Fare was: "Our state population figures are expected to rise sharply when the exodus from Washington, D.C. begins in January."

The September 26 headline was "Clifford Squelches Talk of Troop Cuts." In Mexico City a two day gun battle between soldiers and students killed fifteen. There was a photo of Julie Nixon applauding her sister Tricia holding her son. Chevrolet introduced the 1969 Impala and North Korea released a film showing the crew of the intelligence ship *USS Pueblo* coming ashore with their hands raised in surrender as a narrator said Commander Lloyd M. Bucher was "a criminal who committed espionage." There was a photo of Hank Williams Jr.'s acting debut in *Time to Sing* with Shelley Fabares.

The September 27 paper said that anti war protests were planned for the January 20 inaugural ceremonies. LBJ's nominee for Supreme Chief Justice Abe Fortas was described by a Republican critic as "excessive politicking at its worst." A Republican nominee for Texas Attorney General described the present attorney general, Crawford Martin, as "oozy, squishy, soft on crime." Fowler Fare was: "The Mexico City Olympic Games will be started with a pistol shot... Oh yeah—whose?"

The September 28 headline was the "Cuba Reds Claim CIA Ring Broken." Also on the front page Black Panther leader Huey Newton got two to fifteen years in the death of a white cop. Wray Weddell's column's said that Joske's would begin construction of a shopping center in Northeast Austin after the first of the year. LBJ's son-in-law Airman 1st Class Patrick Nugent was set to become a loadmaster in a C123 in Vietnam. Mussolini's widow was demanding a pension. Barton Pool would close Sunday at eight P.M. and reopen in March, 1969. Kenneth Threadgill was playing the Split Rail. Texas Parks and Wildlife was going to start charging $1 a carload at twenty-four parks.

Michael A. put aside the newspapers after reading Fowler Fare for September 30: "What you could buy for $10 in 1957 now costs $12.19." He only glanced at the cover of Austin's new magazine *The Phoenix:* an unflattering caricature of the University of Texas's Chairman of the Board of Regents Frank Erwin drawn by the Vulcan Gas Company's Jim Franklin. Then he got up from the faded red couch, got a Minimax Grocery brown paper bag from the kitchen and went outside to the garden on the house's west side. Here he paused at what Ryder had written in Marks-A-Lot on the Marvin the Martian scarecrow's helmet:

In memory of Jackson Lamar Brown 1947-1968

"Here comes the kaboom," Michael A. said then set about harvesting the corn ears and placing them in the Minimax Grocery brown paper bag. When finished, he looked at all that remained in the garden—the beans—and was saddened that Bicycle Annie, not Cool Breeze, would tell him when to pick them. This made him recall Cool Breeze quoting Shakespeare the day the two of them had erected the Marvin the Martian scarecrow.

"'Tis an unweeded garden that grows to seed.'"

Michael A. had then said, "Hamlet, Act I, Scene 2" and in that same moment had seen the chimney on the west wall of the house that was almost entirely hidden by vines.

"There's a lot you don't know is here," Cool Breeze had said.

. . .

On that first day of classes Jack learned that both he and Jen had Professors Malof, Ayres, Kruppa and Friedman. This was an even bigger surprise than learning that he, Jen, Taj and Natasha were in the same Early Childhood Education class. Walking home, Jack said to Jen:

"Us being in the same classes don't mean I won't flunk out."

"I'm your longtime gal. I love you. You love me. We love each other and 'Us' is bigger than both of us. Though you smile like a child, you are always my man."

"Are you gonna do my homework?"

"Not all of it."

. . .

On the juke box was Del Shannon's "Runaway" featuring Dave "Baby" Cortez on the organ. By the Chuck Wagon's west wall Taj was holding down the 19th Street kids' table. He had intended to do an advanced calculus problem with his slide rule but had set it aside for one of R.

Crumb's *Zap Comix*. A cartoon character had caught his eye—a big bosomed, big boned hippie chick wearing a T-shirt too small for her, skimpy cutoffs and hiking boots—when he heard:

"Brother, can ya spare a dime?"

Taj looked up and saw a big bosomed, big boned hippie chick wearing a T-shirt too small for her, skimpy cutoffs, and hiking boots. "Sure," he said, digging into pocket.

"They call me Abilene," she said.

"Do you know what a traveler on The Road is, Abilene?"

"Yeah"—taking the money—"a runaway."

. . .

Michael A. was telling himself that no way was he behaving like one of nature's layabouts. He was not even practicing The Fine Art of Hanging Out. He was simply a man-of-no-means-by-no-means on the faded red couch in the living room doing research for his upcoming journey to tie up loose ends.

"I shall use the aliases Maynard G. Krebbs and Gilligan," he said. But then he frowned and said, "Sufferin succotash! I've forgotten Gilligan's first name." For a moment Michael A. pondered and pontificated until he snapped his fingers and said, "I.B. Gilligan." Next he gave himself a thumbs up of approval and said, "Research over. Now I just gotta remember to keep a C-note in my tennie an' bring along my Piegan elkskin medicine bag 'cause ya can't stuff 186K into your jeans'n skivvies." A satisfied Michael A. then curled his godawful ugly toes and stretched out even further on the faded red couch. For a while he admired the treasures strewn about him: his almost new Judy Jetson lunch box, his lava lamp and stack of *Playboys*, the wall posters of Che Guevara's posed corpse in Bolivia, Andy Warhol's Campbell Soup Can and Marlon Brando on his motorcycle in *The Wild One*. Above him on the wall were both the United States flag the honor guard guy had presented to his Ma and another U.S. flag found in the house. With time to kill before *The Uncle Jay Show* on Channel 7, Michael A. was drifting off into a snooze when Maya Karma Gage started bawling her head off.

So off he went into Jack and Jen's bedroom where he stopped stark still at the sight of a teary-eyed Jen covering up her breast and a fussy Maya Karma Gage in her arms.

"She's hungry," Jen said, "but I can't produce milk. Two Moons can and she's promised to help out but she's in class."

"Is it too early for the bottle?"

"Breast milk is best."

Mrs. Medina now came in with a big bosomed, big boned hippie chick wearing a T-shirt too small for her, skimpy cutoffs and hiking boots. "This is Abilene," she said. "Taj sent her. She says she'll wet nurse for a place to stay."

Eyes on Abilene's considerable chest, Michael A. said, "*Just* what the doctor ordered, eh, Jen?"

"Life is timing," Jen said. Then she offered Baby Maya to Abilene and said, "You're on."

"It's Maya who'll be '*on*'," chuckled Michael A.

Abilene next took Baby Maya, pulled up her T-shirt and the infant ceased fussing, even seemed to reach for Abilene's breast.

"Now there's a gal who knows what she wants," Michael A. said. "But hold your horses, Maya. The first thing ya learn is ya got to wait."

"And the second is ya need a place to crash," said Abilene.

"It appears ya just took care of that, darlin'," Michael A. said. Then, eyes big as saucers, he said, "Man oh man, ain't it *udder*ly delightful how Maya's goin' to town?"

Two death stares and one maternal glare of disapproval later Mr. Dynamic Tension left the room in high dudgeon.

. . .

Ryder and Mrs. Smalley were beside the tipi brushing Nachita, Nubia and Monita when a flummoxed Two Moons came home from classes saying, "Chambawamba! Fifteen hours of classes plus a two-hour biology lab, a four-hour chemistry lab and Saturday classes on top of Phys. Ed. three times a week—this sweet little Piegan girl's gonna flunk out!"

"Well, if you do flunk out, there won't be any war for you because females don't get drafted," Ryder said.

Whereupon Mrs. Smalley said, "War! *Hah!* What's it good for? The Great War killed my daddy."

. . .

Michael A., Two Moons and Taj were running errands. First, from Strait Music Company at North Lamar and Tenth Street Taj bought an Altec mixer for their new recording studio. Meanwhile, next door at the S&H Green Stamp Redemption Center, Two Moons used six books of green stamps thrust upon her for school supplies by Mrs. Medina to buy a Friedrich air-conditioner. Next Michael A. drove the pink Cadillac to Grove Drug on Sixth Street where he and Taj waited as Two Moons went inside. When she came out, she had five hundred double ought gelatin caps.

"Now you guys hold up your end of the deal," she said.

"Check," said Michael A. said and put the Caddy in *Drive*. "Soon as we score a Teac reel to reel tape recorder from J.R. Reed Music Company at 805 Congress Avenue it's Hill's Steak House for chicken fried steaks'n cream gravy."

chapter six

Night was closing in on the City of the Violet Crown. It was a little before eight o'clock and on the Monkey Ward's stereo in the 19th Street living room Patsy Cline was singing Willie Nelson's "Crazy." Natasha was walking home from the main library and Taj was just leaving the Engineering Building on his motorcycle. On the front porch Jack and Michael A. sat in the purple butterfly chairs and Abilene was in the bentwood rocker when Ryder came up the porch steps with a 16.75 gallon washtub and set it down in front of them. It was filled with the ears of corn Michael A. had harvested from the garden, supper being Corn and Black Bean Quinoa Salad.

"Nice tub," Michael A. said.

"I found it in the root cellar," Ryder said.

"We got a root cellar?" Jack said.

"Yep," said Ryder, going back down the porch steps.

"You're not gonna help shuck?" said Michael A.

"Nope." Halfway down the steps now.

"No shuck-shuck, no din-din," teased Michael A.

Ryder, now on the walkway, did not reply.

"You're gonna miss tonight's episode of 'The Fugitive'," Jack said as Ryder turned west at the sidewalk.

"Don't ya wanta see what's up with Richard Kimball and his nemesis the one-armed man?" Michael A. said.

"I got my own nemesis," Ryder said and disappeared into the darkness.

"And that's the way it is, September 30th, 1968," said Michael A.

The boys and Abilene then got down to shucking corn, removing the outer leaves from the husk then peeling back the silky threads at the top and pulling off the remaining husk. They had barely begun when a limping Jen came onto the porch with Baby Maya in her arms.

Michael A. said, "Why the gimp, Jen?"

"My ankle aches like the dickens."

Both Jack and Abilene now stood up, Jack taking Baby Maya from Jen and handing her to Michael A. so Abilene could help Jen into the rocker.

"It's swollen and red," Abilene said, taking a look.

Mrs. Medina and Two Moons now came out to see what was going on. As Two Moons took Baby Maya from Michael A., Mrs. Medina said, "Austin gets the Texas Red Spider this time of year and it can do a body damage."

"I killed a reddish brown spider in our bed this morning," Jack said. "That's also when her ankle started hurting."

Mrs. Medina got down on one knee and inspected Jen's ankle. "This is a bad bite," she said. "The veins in her foot are red from the poison."

"What should we do, Ma?"

"Get her to a doctor pronto."

Before Jen could say "Caca pasa, chachalaca," Jack had scooped her up in his arms, Annie was holding open the screen door for them and Two Moons was saying, "Don't fret about Baby Maya, Jen—I'll look after her."

"Where're we going?" Jen said.

"The Health Center," Jack said. After going through the living room, dining room and kitchen with everybody else following, Michael A. got ahead of Jack and Jen to open the screen door while saying:

"It might be better to go to Brackenridge Hospital on 15th Street. The Health Center's all the way over on the University's north side and there's several traffic lights between here and there."

"He's right," Jen said as she and Jack went through the kitchen's screen door.

"Brackenridge it is," Jack said, now going down the back steps. In the driveway and moving toward his pickup, he said, "You drive, Cuz—the key's in it."

"Check," Michael A. said and went to the driver's door of the Fitty Six, opened the door and climbed in to begin goosing the gas pedal while at the same time cranking the 292 cubic inch eight cylinder engine. Seeing the plastic Jesus glued to the center of the dashboard, he said "What the—"

"Yeah, what the—" Jen also said, eyes on the plastic Jesus as Jack helped her into the Fitty Six.

"How did *that* get there?" Jack said as the engine turned over.

. . .

As the Tower clock chimed the first of its eight bells, Taj was headed home. At Littlefield Fountain on 21st Street he turned his Kawasaki 450 motorcycle south onto University Avenue. At 20th Street he maneuvered to the right so a speeding 1968 orange Thunderbird could pass him.

. . .

The Tower clock was chiming its second bell when Jack said to Michael A. as the latter shifted into *Reverse*, "Time's a-wastin'! Step on it."

. . .

The Tower clock was chiming its third bell when Natasha, coming home from her part time job as a page at the main library, walked out of the dark alley that ran south from 21st Street. She had entered 200 West 19th Street's back yard when she saw the Fitty Six's headlights come on. At the same time she became aware of a shadow and a musty odor.

It was then that a life altering and colossal calamity of events for all the 19th Street kids was set in motion.

. . .

As the Tower clock chimed its fourth bell, Michael A. stepped on the gas pedal but did not look back to see if the coast was clear. This was when everybody in the pickup heard a "*Whoa!*" from the sidewalk behind them. The Fitty Six's brakes failed at the same time the man who had yelled "*Whoa!*" dived to safety. "No brakes!" Michael A. yelled as the Fitty Six continued backwards into University Avenue. "Consarned contrap—" was all Jack got to say before everybody's world was stopped by the sound of crashing metal and the shock of impact as the 1968 orange Thunderbird that had sped past Taj clipped the Fitty Six's right rear fender. The collision set the Fitty Six's tires screeching as the pickup spun out of control. Now the Fitty Six was being propelled up University Avenue while the spin's centripetal force kept the three kids inside it pinned to the naugahyde seat. Concurrently, the T-Bird jumped University Avenue's median, bowled over a fire hydrant and a twenty-foot tall geyser erupted.

Natasha, meanwhile, heard none of this because from behind her a forearm had been clamped around her windpipe and someone was forcing her to the ground.

"Uh oh, it's Wiley and Beep Beep's favorite the oak tree," Jen would recall saying as the Fitty Six was about to hit the oak tree head on.

"Yikes! No seat belts! Here comes the kaboom," Michael A. said and extended his right arm to protect Jen from the oncoming impact.

"Brace yourself," Jack said and extended his left arm to protect Jen.

In the meantime Taj was witnessing the wreck when his Kawasaki rode into the fire hydrant's water now flooding the pavement, causing his motorcycle to hydroplane then fall onto its left side, begin sliding along the median's concrete curb. Taj would not remember being dragged along that curb. Nor would Jack, Jen and Michael A. remember the moment that the Fitty Six slammed into the oak tree. They would, however, recall a head peering into each of the Fitty Six's windows. The head at the driver's window belonged to their Gamma Sig neighbor Kilroy who was saying in a drunken slur:

"My old man's gonna be really p.o.'d that you backed into me, Michael A."

"I shorry," Michael A. managed to say. "Braysh fail."

Meanwhile, the head in the passenger side window—soaking wet from the hydrant's water—belonged to the pedestrian who had dived out of the way, a redheaded stranger, forever to be known to the 19th Street kids as Wet Willie.

In the meantime Taj was saying "My arm's numb ..."

... and Natasha' face was pinned to the ground, a voice in her ear saying, "Are you ready for a load of What Goes Bump In The Night, baby?"

chapter seven

No one bothered to call the cops, but someone did call the Water Department to shut off University Avenue's main valve.

The Gamma Sigs who had witnessed the wreck from their front porch knew the 1968 orange T-Bird was Kilroy's and that the Fitty Six was Jack's. They also knew that Kilroy's driver's license was suspended and that more than likely he was drunk, so they were soon on the scene. Two fraternity brothers carried Kilroy away while other brothers heeded Bicycle Annie's orders to push the T-Bird into 200 West 19th Street's garage.

At the same time the drenched redheaded stranger forever to be known as "Wet Willie" was helping Jen get Jack—whose left hip was in great pain—out of the Fitty Six and into the driveway of 200 West 19th Street. Trailing behind them was Mrs. Medina who was helping her son hold his jaw together. Once everybody was in the driveway Bicycle Annie got the injured into the pink Caddy.

Meanwhile, Ryder had come out of nowhere to run up to Taj then sigh and say under his breath "Damn, it's like back on the *Liberty*." Next he helped Taj over to the pink Caddy and into the back seat with Michael A. and Jack.

Bicycle Annie and Mrs. Medina then transported these injured to Brackenridge Hospital.

. . .

Taj's arm was not numb; it was gone, severed by the crash. Ryder retrieved the arm then walked with it the nine blocks to Brackenridge Hospital, but to no avail for Taj was maimed for life. He was a one-armed man.

In the meantime, Michael A. and Jack remained in Brackenridge Hospital overnight for X-rays on the former's broken jaw and the latter's injured left hip. The good news was that Jen was treated and released after being given an antidote for the spider bite that could have killed her. She rode home in the pink Caddy with Bicycle Annie and Mrs. Medina. Once back home Jen limped into her bedroom where Two Moons was nursing Baby Maya. After updating Two Moons, Jen said:

"Did Natasha ever show up?"

"She's in her room. She's pretty freaked out about something."

Jen limped away to find Natasha's door closed, its *Den of Iniquity, enter at your own peril* sign showing for the first time since Natasha had begun sharing Taj's bed. Jen knocked then went inside and found Natasha clutched up on her bed, knees beneath her chin, her hands hiding a face she would not show. Taking the initiative, Jen repeated her update.

"Poor, poor Taj," Natasha sobbed.

"Now tell me what's wrong with you," Jen said and over the next couple of hours the two women built even more on their bond. They held each other and wiped away tears and Natasha decided how she wanted to handle her rape.

"No cops. They'll assume I'm just another loose hippie chick who was asking for it. You can't tell anybody, not even Jack." Natasha then looked at the floor and said, "Man oh man, this could not have come at a worse time."

Jen paused a moment then said, "You mean you might be … ?"

"Fraid so."

. . .

It turned out that Jack's "Brace yourself" warning just before the Fitty Six's collision with the Wiley and Beep's favorite oak tree was a bad idea. When Michael A. held out his right arm to brace Jen for the impact, his left jaw was broken by the pickup's metal steering wheel. Whereas Jack, having stuck his left arm out to brace Jen for impact in the seat-beltless pickup, had also braced himself by firmly planting his feet on the floorboard and this caused his left leg to be rammed into its hip socket. As a result he now walked with a limp.

"Don't fret, hon," he told Jen. "I expect it'll wear off after a while."

chapter eight

On the morning of October 1st Jen left Baby Maya with Mrs. Medina and went to Brackenridge Hospital in the pink Caddy.

There she picked up Jack, Michael A., Taj and his severed arm. They then returned to the scene of the crime—Wiley and Beep Beep's favorite oak tree—and buried Taj's arm beside the dogs' graves. As Taj remained by the oak tree, the limping Jack followed Jen into the garage. There they removed the tarp concealing Kilroy's Thunderbird and saw its only damage was a smashed right headlight. Beside the T-Bird was Jack's baby spit yellow 1956 Ford pickup which obviously had not survived its encounter with the oak tree. Its grille, radiator, fan and engine were a mashed heap of metal.

"My baby's a total loss," Jack said glumly.

"It was only a machine," Jen said. "What you call a 'consarned contraption'. We can recycle the naugahyde seat."

"Yeah, we'll put it on the front porch," Jack said. Then removed the plastic Jesus from the dashboard and said, "This is recyclable too."

"So's this," Jen said and snapped off the Fitty Six's radio antenna.

Taj now joined them to look at his Kawasaki 450 and say, "This too is a total loss."

"Ryder wants to make a sculpture out of it," Jen said.

"Why not?" Jack said and Taj nodded in agreement.

"Well, alrighty then, that's it for termination rituals," Jen said as she dusted off her hands in a dismissive gesture. "Leave us be here now and move on."

. . .

All of Que Tal got into the pink Caddy and, with Jack driving, backed into 19th Street extra carefully. With Dylan's "Rainy Day Women" playing on the eight track stereo they headed west. Passing the north part of Guadalupe Street and seeing congestion at the West Mall's pedestrian crossing, they smiled, glad that they had paid Bicycle Annie to buy their text books. At Lamar they took a right and went to 45th Street. There they made a left turn for the few blocks to Burnet Road. Here they turned right and, after a quick left at the School for the Blind, they parked in front of Big John's House of Crap. Once inside, Michael A. did his greeting ritual with Big John while Jack explained why his cousin's jaw was wired shut and that Michael A.'s shopping list was a globe of the world, a Waring blender for his liquid-only nutrition and wire cutters in case he started choking. Natasha and Taj got six gas heaters and an old-fashioned Maytag washing machine with a ringer for the house. Jen got herself the Ethan Allen boudoir set she wanted. For her, Jack's and Baby Maya's bedroom she got another bentwood rocker. For Maya Karma Gage they got a pink crib, a pink bassinette, pink burping towels, pink stroller, pink play pen and a pink rattle.

"Pink," Jack said. "Everything for Maya's pink."

"That's 'cause she's a girl," Jen said.

"Sounds chauvinistic to me," Jack said.

Afterwards, with the Moontones' 1958 "Book of Love" playing on the pink Caddy's eight track stereo, Que Tal drove to Gulf Mart located further north on Burnet Road at Green Lawn Parkway. Here they got diapers, baby bottles and pacifiers.

For lunch they passed on Kirschner's Café's 85-cent special as well as Mosley's Allandale Cafeteria's "All You Can Eat For Half Price." Instead they partook of the sea food buffet at 5011 Burnet Road where Zuider Zee had all the shrimp you could eat for $2.75. Not Michael A., though; he had fish soup through a straw.

Back home everybody was delighted by Ryder's use of egg cartons to soundproof the White Room.

"Now that new Teac reel to reel recorder can capture Que Tal's sound better," Ryder said.

"Yep, we got us a songcatcher now," said Jack.
"Yeesh," said Michael A, nodding his accord.
"Songcatcher Studio it is then," said Taj.

. . .

On the front porch Taj's Motorola was tuned to Radio KNOW playing "What Now My love" by The Association. Jack was practicing walking with the Piegan walking stick Jolinda Biggs had brought him from La Vaca Lana and Taj was sitting in the purple butterfly chair trying on the Piegan moccasins given him by Daphne.

"Life is change an' life is compromise, Taj," Jack said. "I got one leg shorter than t'other now an' I can't dance country at the Broken Spoke, but I can't get drafted neither."

Taj's reaction was to hold up the *Daily Texan* he was reading and say, "There are 32,155 students enrolled at the University, 19,773 men and 12,382 women."

"Do tell," Jack said then seated himself in the bentwood rocker and took from the waist of his Levis a greasy item wrapped in a brown napkin. "Don't tell Jen about this chili dog Jolinda'n Daphne slipped me," he said.

"No witnesses, no crime," said Taj, smiling.

Jack wolfed down his chili dog then took an envelope from the left back pocket of his Levis while saying, "I got me a letter from Aunt Asilee today." Saying it "Azzlee."

Taj smiled. "A letter from home. I envy you."

"Aunt Asilee's a tough ol' bird. She made me a yellow dog Democrat."

"What is a 'yellow dog Democrat'?"

"Somebody who'd vote for a yellow dog before they'd vote for a Repugnican." Then, opening the letter, he said, "I lived with Aunt Asilee in high school so as not to ride the bus 175 miles from Terlingua to'n from Alpine. Aunt Asilee's got a sheep ranch up in The Hay Stacks but she lives in a rock house on "A" Mountain in Alpine. Life with her was good. We'd eat at The Green Cafe, shop at The Haberdashery an' Morrison's Hardware an' get our groceries from Mr. Martinez or Brun's an' on occasion I'd get my ears lowered at Ramos Barber Shop. Yeah, living with Aunt Asilee was a swell time." Jack then summed up Aunt Asilee's Alpine news for Taj:

"Her arthritis is better now that Doc Lockhart's got her on a new medicine. *The Big Bend Sentinel* says Sul Ross University is building a new library in Alpine an' that November 26 is the dedication of the Harlan J. Smith telescope at the University of Texas McDonald Observatory. Aunt Asilee predicts Robert Halperin'll be a helluva track star an' that it'll be a good year for river reed'n candelilla. Enos Slaughter's getting' spliced to Vashti Mirage an' Alpine's very own Bake Turner's goin' great guns in the NFL … an', wow, talk about not seekin but findin.'"

"Good news?"

"Boy howdy is it." Grinning wide. "Aunt Asilee says that 'cause I'm the first in the family to get a college degree she's givin' me her twenty five sections up in The Hay Stacks."

"Is that not twenty-five square miles?"

"Yep. 160,000 acres. You up for bein' a cowboy, Taj? I'd be proud to have you'n all of Que Tal in on this."

Taj said, "Do you think this one-armed man can ride a horse?"

"Oh hell yeah." Reading on, though, Jack's face fell. "Uh oh. Scooter Culero's MIA in Nam."

"What is 'M' 'I' 'A'?"

"'Missing in action.'"

Taj said nothing. But his gaze was on where his arm had been.

. . .

Tres said to Jack, "So the Wreck of the Fitty Six was a hell of a punch in the gut."

"Yep. Crash, bang—kaboom!"

"We rolled with it," Jen said, "but not without some mubblefubble."

"Nobody chooses the sunrise nor picks the sunset," Tres said.

chapter nine

Later that Tuesday, October 1st, Michael A. was on the faded red couch in the living room doing some pondering. First he decided to tease his hair, give it more body should Natasha and Jen's snarky gibe that he was developing male pattern baldness be true. Regarding his wired-shut jaw, he decided to delay tying up loose ends in the Nacho-Tunoose gig and that his primary goal would be getting his jaw unwired in time for the Halloween party. Pondering some more, he decided against any possible conflicts with their fellow counterculture capitalists down at the Vulcan Gas Company. Therefore Purple People Eater Productions would show movies only on Mondays, Tuesdays or Wednesdays. He further decided that from now until Halloween the movies for Purple People Eater would be horror flicks like tonight's *The Beast With Five Fingers* at the Academic Center Auditorium. Next he cogitated that Maynard G. Krebbs' favorite movie *The Monster That Ate Cleveland* was not a real flick. Michael A. then began perusing today's movie ads. *Fanny Hill Meets Dr. Erotica* was at the Capri, *Prudence and the Pill* was showing at the State, Boris Karloff's *Die, Monster, Die* was at the Burnet Road Drive In. Boris was also in *Black Sabbath* at the Austin Theatre at 3900 South Congress. Michael A. then read an article about a new horror flick called *Night of the Living Dead* that had been made for only $114,000. This led him to ponder about making his own movie, a "based on a true story" flick about how 200 West 19th was a haunted house. Next the other Austin houses he had lived in came to mind. He was thinking he would check them out when Natasha thunder-stomped up to him in her combat boots and said:

"Poor baby. Feelin' sorry for yourself 'cause your jaw is wired shut an' you're hankering for a Mooreburger'n fries? Well, no pity party for Mikey A. Get past it. Be creative." Next she tossed a Big Chief tablet and Marks-A-Lot at him, said "Be all you can be, spitbird" and left.

Pissed off yet inspired, Michael A. picked up the Big Chief and Marks-A-Lot and drew a caricature of her.

. . .

October 2, a Wednesday. The headline was "Johnson Staying With Fortas." There was a photo of a shirtless and hairy Jerry Rubin Yippie in silent protest before a House subcommittee investigating the Chicago riots. In Vietnam 901 war planes had been shot down so far. The state sales tax would rise to 4%. The Good Humor Band was at The New Orleans Club. The Sweetarts were at the Jade Room. For 99 cents The Sizzler at 7414 Guadelupe would sell you a half pound of good ground round plus baked potato with all the fixins and garden fresh salad. The Stallion drive-in had 15-cent barbeque on a bun plus chips. They also had 35-cent fried chicken. All the tacos you could eat were at Murphy's in Hancock center for 88 cents. Channel 12 had *Cat Ballou* at 11.

Meanwhile, showing on the Scho Pro Lounge television set was the first game of the World Series between the St. Louis Cardinals and Detroit Tigers with Curt Gowdy and Harry Caray broadcasting. On the table nearest to the TV was a stack of $1 coupons without expiration dates, a pitcher of beer, a box of straws and three mugs. It was Taj's first baseball game.

"Baseball is a team sport played without a clock, yes?"

"Yeah," Jack said, "an' it ain't over 'til somebody wins."

"Jus' 'ike 'ife," said Michael A. then sucked down some beer.

. . .

Once he and Ryder had moved the Fitty Six's naugahyde seat to the front porch, Jack said, "How about a Mooreburger?"

"No thanx. I just had a grackle."

Jack frowned. "You're kidding, right?"

"Okay." Not giving it much.

A little later Jack said to Jen, "Ryder's gonna paint the T-Bird Maya blue."

Jen said, "Cool. He's a handy guy. But do we really know him?"

"Not yet. But both Cool Breeze'n Tunoose vouched for him."

"He bought a dozen generic T-shirts and Jolinda and Daphne said all of 'em are the one that says *Based on an actual event*."

. . .

Ryder was in the garage pondering how to make what he called a "hideosity" out of the bed of the Fitty Six and Taj's Kawasaki when Two Moons came in and said:

"Why didn't you come home after you got out of the Navy?"

Ryder did not hesitate. "Because I was a mess an' I didn't want the tribe to see me like that. Also a radio operator hears everything, so I figured they'd be looking for me an' The Rez'd be the first place they'd look. I'd heard Austin was a cool place to learn to be a jeweler, so I hitchhiked here."

"And how'd the Piegans' Jeweler Bob become Ryder?"

"'Ryder' was the name on an army shirt I found."

"So why do you always wear the same T-shirt?"

"It's therapeutic."

"I can see how it would be. Anyway, the tribe's real proud of you. Both the Navy part and the Que Tal part."

"Life's a trip. There I am about to be rousted by Cool Breeze for floppin' on the front porch when he sees my army shirt an' decided to take in a fellow vet. Then I hear Walks In Blue Green's captain was Michael A.'s pa an', bim bam boom, now we're all gettin' well."

"Yep, we got so much money to burn I wanta buy a bike."

"Natasha's quit ridin' her Honda so why not ask her about it."

"I will, if she'll talk to me." After a pause she said, "Walks In Blue Green's stoked about My Lai. He says it'll end the war which is, what? Almost five years old?"

"My war lasted only four days," Ryder said. "By the way, my poking around tells me there was once a privy by your tipi. Be easy to resurrect it if ya want."

"Cool." She was quiet a moment before saying, "Umm, just exactly what're you 'poking around' for?"

"Wampum. Any kind of wampum."

chapter ten

Maya Karma Gage slept through her first visit to the limestone grotto in Waller Creek. Right now she was looking cute as a bug in her pink stroller while snoozing to Radio KNOW playing Jimi Hendrix's "All Along the Watchtower" on Taj's borrowed orange Motorola transistor radio. Next to her, Jack and Jen sat on the concrete bench that was a memorial to a daughter lost to polio in 1952.

"This bench is a reminder to get Maya vaccinated," Jen said.

"I asked a nurse in Brackenridge about that," Jack said. "She's gonna fix us up with a good pediatrician."

Jen grinned. "You're going to be a good father, Ben Jack Gage."

"I'll be tryin' my durn bestest right up to my last breath."

"Remember the first thing we learned in Early Childhood Education class?"

"Yep. Parenting is the least developed skill."

Jack then stood up and limped over to the oak tree up which their dogs Wiley and Beep had once chased a squirrel. Meanwhile, Jen began humming a tune as she took out cucumber sandwiches and Mayapan couscous from her Maya rucksack. When she saw Jack lean against the tree James Dean style to clean his fingernails with his Case knife, the pose told her he had something on his mind. When he put away his knife, she was ready for him.

"You know what, hon?"

"What, Ben Jack Gage?"

"A feller once told me 'Dream as if you're gonna live forever but live as if you're gonna die today."

"I recall you telling me that."

"I told you that before?"

"At least a dozen times. James Dean told it to you'n the other kids on the set of the movie *Giant*."

"Well, I still think it's worth mentioning."

"Really? You think 'live as if you're gonna die today' is a good attitude for a parent?"

"Oops." Then he brightened and said, "Nawww, but I'm here to tellya Elizabeth Taylor sure had pretty eyes."

"They were sapphire like mine, weren't they?"

"They still are."

"Jaaack?"

"Yeah?"

"Are we gonna get married here?"

"Here in Austin?"

"No, in the grotto."

"Beats me. Women are in charge of weddings."

"Glad to hear it". Winking at him. "And that reminds me that I need to get you to go along on a coupla wedding details."

"Lets hear 'em."

"Can we have a small wedding outdoors? A private ceremony? Nobody but us and the preacher?"

"No best man?" Jack grinned. "Still don't cotton to Michael A., do ya?"

Jen winced. "Oh, I like him a little bit, but not much 'cause, well, he has proven to be somewhat shifty."

"Shifty? Cuz? Oh hell yeah he's shifty." Then Jack thought a moment and said, "An' I spose the other thing you'd like to get me to go along on is a wedding ring?"

"Now, Ben Jack Gage, don't you go trying to pull the rug out from under me on this. If I got a ring on the third finger of my left hand I'll remember our wedding every blessed day." Jen then reached into the

AUSTINTACIOUS: A Tale of 1968 Austin

pocket of her cutoffs to bring out a slip of paper and say, "Here's the ring size. You're a rich 'un, so don't be chintzy. Ya hear?"

"Yes, ma'am."

. . .

Natasha went downstairs to what was now Mrs. Medina's room and said, "Will you please tell me what my was mother like?"

After giving it some thought, Mrs. Medina said, "I only knew Chanil in the strife and struggle that was the refugee camp. She was a beautiful soul, also my sister in arms and sorrow. There was no stronger person." Then she smiled and said, "I've told you that you are the spitting image of her, but now that I know you better I see that you are almost the lady herself."

"And my father?"

"There is nothing I can tell you other than what your mother told me."

"What was that?"

"That he called her 'the love of his life' and that she was sure she was his. I once asked what he was like. Her reply was to give me a coy smile and say, 'Oh, like any man, only more so.'"

Natasha now saw the Tarot deck in Mrs. Medina's apron pocket and said, "Will you do a reading for me?"

Mrs. Medina agreed and once the reading over she said, "Now I am even more awed at how much you resemble your mother."

. . .

Across the street Mrs. Smalley was blasting away with her shotgun which was her way of scaring off the grackles in her pecan trees. Meanwhile, Taj sat on the north window sill of his bedroom with a face he would not show. He felt as low as when he had been struck mute. The Wreck of the Fitty Six had diminished his being. He could no longer be the drummer he once was nor could he ride a motorcycle or drive a car. He could not even go up to the Crow's Nest. And the sight of his leather slide rule scabbard with **TAJ** neatly written on it in black Marks-A-Lot made him doubt he could still become an engineer, much less have a career with the National Aeronautics and Space Administration.

Taj wished the Texas Medicine would soon kick in so he could at least visualize himself up in the Crow's Nest flying the Purple Crab kite and visiting with Boo Boo—"*Cheep!*"—the chick.

Despair now bowed his head and shut his eyes, made him shake his head and wonder what his mother would say about his newest disability. He knew what his father would say, a thought that prompted Taj to open his eyes and look down to see Ryder milking the goats in front of Two Moons' tipi. Even the sight of Ryder chasing off some grackles did not amuse Taj. Losing his left arm meant that just getting dressed was a chore. To avoid shaving, he had decided to grow a beard. Though he would wear only T-shirts, pants with elastic waists and eschew skivvies, chanclas were a tough task and his Piegan moccasins lacked in cold temps. He missed his desert boots. It was tough to tote his colorful Maya rucksack.

He thought: What a year this 1968 has been. I make friends with good people, live in a wonderful home, I am in a band, I get my voice back … then I lose my arm … and no arm means no drumming which means no gigs for Que Tal … Natasha has dumped me and speaks only to Jen. Maybe I should run off to the circus.

Now shaking his head, Taj leaned out the window to see Ryder crawl under the back porch. But then behind him Taj heard a "meow" and turned around to see, beside the open door of his closet, both Hannah and Boo Boo.

"This is new," he said, wondering how they got there.

It was then that Boo Boo announced with a "*pwaaak!*" that she was no longer a chick and a nonchalant Hannah extended her front legs in a stretch to say hello. The cat then sat on her haunches to groom herself by licking her left paw and using it to wash her face while Boo Boo began to cluck and search the floor for chicken scratch. Now the Texas Medicine kicked for Taj and he started to hallucinate he was eight miles high over Akumal Bay and admiring the bay's never-ending waves head for ashore … and within this dream state the inkling of an idea arrived.

"Wave power," he said to himself. "Connectivity via biomimicry is CoEvolution."

It was then that Natasha opened the door to look in and say in her direct way, "You're a smart guy and you'll figure it out. Life is change, life is compromise. Stop feeling sorry for yourself and get on with your life. Be here now, Bridge Beyond the Light. Cope with your new normal."

"But, Dawn Song, won't you even tell me what is wrong between us?"

"Nope," she said and closed door.

A moment later Two Moons came to the door and said, "Ryder wants to know when it'd be okay to start on getting you back up into the Crow's Nest."

chapter eleven

On October 3rd, a Thursday, the headline was "Release of Guard Reserves Planned," the National Guard having been called up after the *USS Pueblo* incident. Other news: LBJ withdrew his nomination of Abe Fortas as chief justice after the Senate failed to end a filibuster against the nomination; the Democrats said a letter stating that Hubert Humphrey would meet with George Wallace was fake; ex Cuban dictator Batista blamed the U.S. for his ouster; Twiggy weighed 92 pounds and her measurements were 31-23-31; Channel 12's movie at 11 was *Behind the Iron Curtain*; Marcel Duchamps, the "father of poo art" and painter of "Nude Descending a Stairway" in 1913, died at age 81; CBS's Morley Safer said a photographer for *Time Life* was killed by sniper in Biafra; there was a photo of Princess Grace and Prince Rainier at Hemisfair in San Antonio; Shirley Temple Black had showed her bandaged right hand to an admirer at Hemisfair; and banks were now charging 6% interest. There was also a photo of Georgia's governor riding a bicycle backwards.

Meanwhile, in the Scho Pro Lounge, on a table near the TV were five $1 coupons next to five pitchers. In the hand of each Que Tal member was a mug. After Detroit evened the World Series at a game a piece, Taj placed his mug on the table and said:

"It is obvious I can no longer be your drummer and no drummer means no gigs, so I now withdraw from Que Tal."

Michael A. set his mug down hard on the table and said, "*Noosh! Noosh!*"

"There will be no Que Tal without Taj," Jen said and set down her mug next to Michael A.'s.

"Forever us. Us *forever!*" Jack said and set his mug beside the others.

"Ever forward with one for all and all for one," Natasha said and also placed her mug with the others.

Michael A. next used the Marks-A-Lot and the white vinyl clipboard Taj had given him to write *Family first!* then hold it up for all to see.

"Michael A. is a good guy to have liking you," Taj said, clearly moved.

. . .

At dinner that night a toss of the I Ching confirmed Que Tal's decision to make Aunt Asilee's 160,000-acre sheep ranch in The Hay Stacks part of Xutan Partners' holdings. And Natasha's suggestion to add goats to the sheep ranch—"I was raised on goat's milk"—made Jack even more proud.

"Well alrighty then," he said, nodding. "We're gonna feed'n clothe folks."

Next Jack put forward a proposal from Mrs. Medina that Xutan Partners purchase the small houses of her three church ladies so they could afford an old age home.

"The houses are downtown property an' the price is right," Jack said. "There're also near the court house so, in exchange for free legal services, they can be offices for Cousin Brucie an' friends. We're talking a real estate lawyer, a tax lawyer an' one who specializes in filing law suits against Uncle Sam."

"Jackpot," said Taj, nodding. "Bees, hummingbirds, here comes your $30 billion."

"It's too bad none of our new lawyers is an entertainment lawyer," Jack said, "'cause Que Tal's gonna need one."

. . .

Later that night was the first band practice in Songcatcher Studio, also Que Tal's first time to play together since the Wreck of the Fitty Six.

There were some innovations: Two Moons and Abilene sat in on the session, Two Moons on tom tom and Abilene on washtub bass, the latter a Ryder product. Ryder had taken the 16.75 gallon washtub he had found in the root cellar and upended it to attach a four-foot-long-one-inch-in-diameter dowel and ten feet of quarter inch rope. Then he had used some hardware to make it into a washtub bass. The added percussion and bass produced an electric-jug sound which made the beat laid down by Que Tal both crisper and fuller. A surprise came when Que Tal heard the Teac reel to reel's recording of the session: Taj had been singing along and, even better, he could carry a tune.

"Lordy, Taj," Jack said, "you sound like Roy Orbison."

"There's some Jim Morrison in there too," Jen said.

An inspired Que Tal then worked up Roy Orbison's "Only the Lonely" and The Doors' "Light My Fire."

. . .

After band practice Michael A. went to the church-door-turned-dining-room table and counted the money in the three lock box. He was stunned at the amount of moolah Que Tal had amassed. Reminded of what a boon it was to have had Nacho for a grandfather, he looked over at the floor-to-ceiling bookcase and the terracotta statuette there, the one that Nacho had given Que Tal. The statuette had a round base on which six figurines stood in a circle, each figurine's arms extended, a hand resting on the shoulder of the adjacent figurine. For some reason a Maya riddle popped into Michael A.'s head:

"Why does the wolf howl at the moon?"

Then he heard Mona say, "Because a wolf can't sing."

And then that bell rang again.

chapter twelve

On October 4, a Friday, Jen was in her bedroom reading the paper. She was by the front porch window in the new bentwood rocker from Big John's. She read about a student at Austin's McCallum High School being expelled for long hair. She read that third party presidential candidate George Wallace had chosen retired Air Force Chief of Staff Curtis LeMay as his running mate and that, when asked about his position on the use of nuclear weapons, LeMay said, "It's just another weapon… there are many times when it would be efficient to use." Bill Mauldin's cartoon was a Heil Hitler salute with the caption "It can happen here." The caption to a photo of a captured student in Mexico City's student riots said twenty-five people had been killed and one hundred wounded. Jen saw that four more Fort Hood soldiers had been charged with disobedience at the Chicago riots, making a total of twenty-four. She was turning the page when she heard:

"Hello in the house."

Lowering the paper, Jen looked out the window and saw Kilroy on the front porch. He had on a starched white button-down collar short-sleeve shirt, red madras shorts and penny loafers.

"We were expecting you," Jen heard Natasha say to Kilroy. Natasha was in one of the purple butterfly chairs, her fine long legs up, her knees beneath her chin. She wore a white tank top, cutoffs and her combat boots.

"Hubba hubba," Kilroy said at the sight of her then collected himself and said, "I must discuss recompense with Michael A."

"Michael A. can't discuss. His jaw's wired shut."

"Oh, I didn't know that. Not from the wreck I hope."

"Sure 'nough *was* from the wreck."

"Well, it's his own fault."

"You were speeding. Taj will swear to that."

"Michael A. backed into me."

"Jack's pickup is a total loss too."

"But Michael *A*. backed into *meee*."

Natasha said, "The whole thing was a calamity of events set in motion by brake failure. Because you were speeding, Taj had to let you pass him. Then you ran over the fire hydrant which then flooded the street and caused Taj to lose his arm."

"Holy moly! Nobody told me he lost his arm."

"You were drunk. We have witnesses."

"Oh, my."

"We covered up for you by hiding your vehicle."

Clearly flustered, Kilroy said, "Look, just keep the T-Bird and we'll let bygones be bygones."

"Nope. No way. The T-Bird's been reported stolen." Then, giving him a dead eyes glare, she said, "Our lawyer says he's going to file charges against you. Drunk driving, bodily injury, property loss. He wants to file a law suit too. And of course at the trial your history as a masher will have to come out."

"Can money make this go away? Say a grand?"

"$1250. Cash money. Which is way cheaper than a DWI not to mention bodily injury and property loss."

Kilroy frowned. "Are you a business major?"

"Nope."

"Pre law?"

"I started out as a Philosophy major then Poly Sci but now I'm Undeclared. All I know for sure is that one must be very careful in this dog-eat-dog world."

Kilroy closed his eyes. "$1250 it is."

"Now aren't you just *tooo* sweet." Smiling some.

Kilroy said, "But I must suggest something be done for all concerned. Since the T-Bird's been reported stolen, have it painted a different color." Then he winked and said, "Some license plates off another '68 T-Bird would be good too."

"Good thinking," Natasha said then batted her eyes and said, "I hear Blues Boy Hubbard is playing your Gamma Sig party tomorrow night."

"Yes, he is."

"Is Que Tal invited?"

"By all means," he said then got out of there and right after was when Jen said through her window:

"Natasha? Who, pray tell, was that masked woman who just railroaded Kilroy?"

"That was Nasty Nat doing damage control."

. . .

October 5. At Gamma Sig's gig Kilroy gave Natasha $1250 cash money, the keys to the 1968 T-Bird and a package.

"What's in the package, Kilroy?"

"License plates." Then Kilroy pointed to a fellow across the room and said, "They're his. Being your usual self involved oily, George won't even notice they're gone."

Natasha said, "What's an 'oily'?"

"An oil rich scion. Somebody born with a silver spoon in his mouth, has everything given to him." Then Kilroy winked and said, "How's about me'n Que Tal having a talk about making it in the music bidness?"

"Later, gator," she said and headed for Oily George.

. . .

They were all tipsy and Kilroy was saying to Taj, Michael A., Jack and Jen, "The oil bidness has been good to me'n mine but the music bidness beckons the entrepreneur in me. So I say let rock rule—I wanta be your lawyer."

"Das okay wit me," said Michael A., smiling his sly smile.

"Ditto," Jen said, winking.
"Cool," Jack said, nodding.
"I concur," Taj said.
"We could start with a radio commercial," Kilroy said.
"Actually," said Taj, "we could create our own radio station if we had a transmitter."
"Gettin' a transmitter's no problem," Kilroy said. "When the Brits banned rock music on the BBC, my old man bought a piece of a pirate radio station that broadcasts from the English Channel."

. . .

The next afternoon Jen finally got sick and tired of Jack fooling around, so she said to him over her left shoulder:
"Willya quit fidgeting around back there? Mrs. Medina can't mind Baby Maya all day'n I'm good to go so *let's git!*"
"Hold your horses, hon."
"Why? What's the hold up? Your Piegan walking cane?"
"Nawww. And it ain't a cane. It's a *stick*."
"Then what's the problem?"
"I cain't get comfortable."
"It's no different back there than being on a bicycle."
"But it just don't *feeel* right."
"It'll be okay, Jack. Just reach around and take hold of me."
"My gut instincts say this is against the Laws of Nature, Jen. I'm wayyy too big for you this way. I shouldn't be back here. This ain't natural."
"MCP," she said and revved the Triumph's engine.
"I ain't no male chauvinist pig. No way!"
"We're doing this to save the planet, Jack."
"The high price of fossil fuel's got somethin' ta do with it too. Lawwwsy mercy! 35 cents a gallon! What's the world comin' to?" Then, fidgeting some more, he said, "I got a sneakin' suspicion I'll get throwed off."
"All that's being thrown off is your male ego. Now sit still on your"—using a teasing tone—"pussy pad."

"'Bitch bench' is whut I heard it called."

"Oh, piffle. Willya just hush up'n put your arms around my hips? Before you know it Cowboy'll be cooling off in Barton Springs's sixty-eight degree water." She revved the Triumph's engine then eased off and said, "Jaaack?"

"Whut?"

"Lower your hands. They're not on my hips."

"No ma'am, they ain't." Sounding perky. "I'm startin' ta see how a feller could like it back here."

Jen then muttered about life being compromise and popped the clutch, Jack held on tight and they roared out of the driveway. At University Avenue's stop sign Jen headed west on 19th Street. At Lamar they went south before again turning west on Barton Springs Road. Jen rode so well and did Jack so proud he said:

"Like Cool Breeze said, hon, you're an empowered gal."

. . .

After their dip in Barton Springs, Jen said to Jack, "Wanta window shop for a new vehicle?"

"Oh hell yeah I do."

Jen wanted their first stop to be Covert Buick Company at 500 West 5th because it was Covert's 57th year in business and they were having a Riviera sale. But Jack objected, saying:

"A Riviera ain't a family vehicle, hon."

Next was Simmons Motor Company at 12th and Lamar where a Corvette caught Jen's eye. But again Jack objected, saying:

"Too conspicuously consumptive, Jen. A talisman of the leisure class won't work for a family of three." Then he heard The Who's "Magic Bus" on a passing vehicle's radio and said, "Let's head over to 405 North Lamar."

"What's over there, Jack? A lipstick pickup like the Fitty Six?"

"Way better'n that."

The salesman at C.B. Smith Volkswagen was a sharp cookie who, sizing up Jack and Jen as hippies, showed them a light blue Volkswagen bus. Jack looked at its engine, kicked its tires, used his finger to check for oil residue in the exhaust then he and Jen took a test drive. Afterwards, Jen agreed when Jack said:

"This is without a doubt the best durned consarned contraption for us."

"I could tell you took a fancy to Cacciatore's VW bus when we were in Douglas, Arizona," Jen said. Then, taking a wad of three -lock-box hundred dollar bills out of her hippie purse, she said, "Now we just dicker down the price a bit."

"Cash is king," Jack said.

. . .

They bought the VW bus for $2200 then loaded up the Triumph and drove seven blocks to the gas station at 12th and Lamar.

"I bet it'll take less than five bucks to fill 'er up," Jack said to the attendant. "An' no need to check the water 'cause it's an air cooled engine." Next, as the attendant washed the windows and checked the oil, Jack and Jen stood off to one side to admire their purchase, Jack saying:

"You know what, hon?"

"What?"

"Earl Scheib over on East Second says he'll paint any car any color for $55."

"Does ol' Earl have Maya blue?"

"I betcha he could come up with it. An' how'd it be if we personalize it some. Maybe get Michael A. to paint a peace sign over the raised VW logo on the front an' on each headlight he draws a black hand with the fingers hanging down?"

"Ouuu, yeaaah." Getting into it. "Then the front of the bus would look like a monster."

"Be a scary sight in anybody's rear view mirror," Jack said and went to pay the gas tab. When he came back and got behind the wheel, he said, "She topped off at four dollars and forty cents."

"Cool," Jen said. "But have you noticed the license tag?"

"No. Why?"

"It says 'O-U-I-2-L-S-D.'"

"So?"

"That's 'Yes to LSD.'"

"Hmmm." Frowning. "That might give a cop reason to pull over a tricked out Maya blue hippie van that looks like a monster in the rear view mirror."

"Well, this *is* just a bus, just a tool really, and no paint job or monster frills will help this consarned contraption run any better."

"Okay, so we leave her be," Jack said. "But I'm still personalizing the new baby a wee eensy snitch."

And once they were back home Jack glued the Fitty Six's plastic Jesus on the VW's dashboard.

chapter thirteen

"Jaaack?"

"Yes, hon?"

"Where are we now?"

"Still rolling down Interstate 20, hon. We're maybe an hour west of Abilene."

"Oh," she said, "What they call 'The Big Country'." Then Jen looked down at the shoe box on her lap holding the black-and-white snapshots of her and Jack's time in 1968 at 200 West 19th Street in Austin. Without looking up, she said, "Do you know about the Weatherman, Tres?"

"George Carlin's Hippy Dippy Weatherman bit? From the Smothers Brothers Show DVD you gave me?"

"I always liked George Carlin," Jen said, still not looking up. "He was on KXOL in 1959. He was stationed at Carswell."

"Carswell?" Tres said. "The place we're going?"

"Back then it was a military base."

"Oh. So who was the Weatherman?"

Jen stayed quiet so Jack answered. "In the '1960s homegrown terrorism was something else that didn't have a name yet. The Weatherman was a faction of the Students for a Democratic Society. In 1969 they bombed establishment symbols like Bank of America, the U.S. Capitol building, the Pentagon. Natasha got sucked in an' it got her life in prison. She escaped an' hid out in a missile silo, but eventually she got nabbed down along the Rio Grande."

Tres said, "Nobody else in Que Tal was into homegrown terrorism?"

"Nope, our calling was dabbling in the underground economy."

"And you made a bundle. What was your business model?"

"Save fifty percent, invest thirty percent an' keep twenty percent to live on. We'd make a pile then launder it, bank it 'n live off the interest. Nacho, Tunoose an' Rosko set us up an' as it turned out we were in the right place at the right time. We also had luck an' diversity 'cause, like Milo Minderbinder in Catch 22, Michael A. has a financial mind an' Taj has a wunderkind gift for practical wisdom. The music kept us together an' gave us hippie values like 'share an' share alike' an' it didn't hurt that the vast majority of our market—our fellow baby boomers—was half the population an' had twenty billion bucks they were only too willing to spend irresponsibly."

Tres said, "Like a lot of baby boomers, you made enough money to buy Miami. But you didn't piss it away."

"Though Que Tal was a proud bunch, we learned that pride can be your greatest strength or your greatest weakness."

Jen said, "Therefore we fought the good fight against self magnification."

. . .

It was the darkness before dawn and in Songcatcher Studio all of Que Tal plus Bicycle Annie were euphoric after an inspirational practice.

It was also Annie's first all-nighter with the band and she was glowing with euphoria. Seeing this, Jack said to her with a sly smile:

"Was it Texas Medicine that kept you up all night, Annie?"

"No sirree." Grinning. "Twas y'all's music. It's perk'n pluck make this old biddy giddy'n flat out high on life."

"We *were* good tonight, weren't we?" Natasha said.

"Yesssh!" said Michael A., pumping his fist in the air.

"And you were great, Taj," Jen said. "You still got it."

"Yes. Perhaps I can still be Que Tal's drummer."

"We all believe that," Jack said, "an' I'm for celebratin' by taking a spin up to Austin's best sunrise."

. . .

"'Og," said Michael A. as Que Tal and Bicycle Annie looked out the kitchen door at a pre dawn fog.

"A cloud serpent," Taj said to Natasha.

"We shall rise above it," said Jen.

"Onward through the fog," Jack said, going out the door.

Soon the VW bus was backing out of the driveway, all eyes within making sure nothing was speeding their way. They took a right onto 19th Street and drove past The Drag then Lamar Boulevard to Exposition Boulevard. There they took another right and went north to West 35th Street. After a left turn, they went west and upward a few blocks and turned into an empty parking lot. Here they exited the VW bus and scaled a stairway's hundred stone steps. They had climbed above the dull gray cloud serpent, but they could not see Lake Austin snaking its way toward town nor make out the hill country to the south, west and north of them.

"Bummer," said Natasha, looking north. "I wanted to see Jollyville. That's where I was raised on goat's milk. We were cedar choppers, folks who—"

And in that moment Natasha and everyone else was struck dumb with wonder as, behind them, in the east, Father Sun was shooting daybreak through the sky: blazing a streak of sunrise that parted the cloud serpent.

"As is sky so is earth and sea," said Taj.

"So say la maya," said Jen.

"The Forces That Are have brewed yet another calamity of events," said Natasha.

"Who says you can't choose the sunrise?" said Jack.

"So say la maya," said Bicycle Annie.

"Wun p'anet, wun worl'!" said Michael A., his imagination conjuring up images of Niagara falls, a cornice of cumulus, the Milky Way, the Grand Canyon, the Starship *Enterprise* encountering a Klingon warship amidst Q-tips, puffed Quaker Oats, Sahara beaches, sand dunes beside a shoreline, Antarctica's icey-blue bayous.

Meanwhile, Jack and Jen were seeing Santa Elena Canyon.

And Taj and Natasha were seeing an azure blue drop-off beyond a continental shelf of white powder sand.

As daybreak now dappled them in orange and white, Bicycle Annie gave some historical perspective, saying, "Welcome to Mount Bonnell, an Austin landmark and at an elevation of 785 feet the tip-top of the City of the Violet Crown. Named for George W. Bonnell who fought for Texas's independence in 1836. In 1839, as head of Indian Affairs, he moved to Austin and started *The Austin Sentinel*. In 1898 a woman named Hazel went sliding down a cable from this summit into Lake Austin which was then called Lake McDonald." Annie then paused before saying:

"I now see you young whippersnappers as family. An' that's like daybreak in your head. It rattles the bones of the dead."

chapter fourteen

On October 10 the Detroit Tigers won the World Series. After the last out, Jen looked at the guys then turned to Natasha and said: "Have you picked up on it too?"

"I think so." Natasha then looked at Jack and said, "Droopy mustache, ponytail." Next she looked at Taj and said, "Scraggly beard, frizzy hair." Then she looked at Michael A. and said, "Brillo hair, round face." To Jen she said, "Life imitating art, right?"

"You got it. We live'n play with Freewheelin' Franklin Freek, Phineas Phreak and Fat Freddy Freekowski."

"Our own Fabulous Furry Freak Brothers," Natasha said.

"You neglected to mention Fat Freddy's cat," said Taj.

Que Tal then grinned as one and clinked their mugs together and said in five part harmony, "Ever forward."

"While knowing full that nothing lasts forever," said Jen.

. . .

That same Thursday New Atlantis and Johnny Winter played the one-year anniversary of The Vulcan Gas Company at 316 Congress Avenue. Houston White, Don Hyde, Sandy Lockett, Gary Maxwell and artist Jim Franklin had converted the W.B. Smith building, formerly a dry goods store opened in 1884, into a rock music venue. The Vulcan had homemade benches and an elevated light show emanating from a suspended platform accessible via a trap door in the ceiling. It had no liquor license because one of the guys had been convicted of selling acid to a nark. Admission was $1.50.

. . .

On October 11 Apollo 7 was launched for an eleven-day-163-orbit journey around Earth.

. . .

On October 16, with Thelma and Barney Lou and family watching from their fishbowl atop the Stromberg Carlson television set, Michael A., his mother, Abilene and Baby Maya were having lunch at the church-door-turned-dining room table. Ma was waiting to watch "As the World Turns" and having some of the Waring blender's strained peas she had made for her son. Abilene was eating a peanut butter sandwich and Baby Maya was going full tilt boogie on Abilene's breast. Right there leering at the latter was Michael A. taking his lunch through a straw, the new *Playboy* open on his lap. He showed the fold-out to Abilene and said:

"'ut ouu tink?"

Abilene looked, winced and said, "That poor victim of male chauvinism can't hold a candle to me."

As Michael A. nodded in agreement, Ma said, "I never should've bought you that first *Playboy*. 'Art' my Aunt Fanny—it's just another dirty magazine."

It was then that an update about the Olympics in Mexico City came on the Stromberg Carlson television set. American track stars John Carlos and Tommy Smith had placed first and second in the 200 meter sprint and were on the awards stand to get their medals. When the "Star Spangled Banner" began, both athletes bowed their heads and thrust a clenched fist into the air—the salute for Black Power. Whereupon Michael A. jumped to his feet and said:

"Yesssh! etter dan i-yackin plane ta Cuba!"

Whereupon his Ma grabbed the wire cutters from her son's pocket and said, "Don't worry! Mother will save her little man!"

"Chill, Mrs. Medina," Abilene said. "Your boy's cheering, not choking."

In the meantime, Baby Maya missed nary a drop of lunch.

. . .

At the Vulcan Gas Company on October 17 it was Shiva's Head Band plus Johnny Winter.

. . .

On October 20th on the private island of Skorpios Jacqueline Kennedy became Mrs. Aristotle Onassis.

. . .

It was Sunday, October 27. Daylight Savings Time was over and Taj had just taken his first step onto the Ryder-built spiral stairway connecting Taj's north bedroom window to the Crow's Nest.

"I cannot thank you enough, Ryder."

"There was one like it on the *Pueblo*."

"Whoa! You were on the *USS Pueblo*?"

"Yep. Transferred out before the North Koreans captured her."

"You were lucky."

"About the *Pueblo*, yeah." Ryder then said, "You think anybody'd mind if I borrow a saxophone I found in the attic?"

"I doubt anyone would mind," Taj said. He was wondering why Ryder had been in the attic when Ryder said:

"I figure the sax is probably from when this was a music academy."

"Highly likely," Taj said, now wondering how Ryder knew the 19th Street house had been a music academy.

. . .

During dinner—Balsamic Root Vegetable from La Vaca Lana's Oedibles deli plus fresh baked bread and tortillas from Mayapan—Bicycle Annie said:

"Two years ago today, October 29, 1966, the Thirteenth Floor Elevators appeared on Dick Clark's American Bandstand to lipsynch their Top Forty hit "You're Gonna Miss Me." Afterwards, Dick Clark asked who the head of the band was and that stinker Tommy Hall said 'We're all heads, man.'"

Everybody cracked up but Two Moons, so Ryder said to her, "A 'head' is Austin hippie slang for someone who smokes pot."

"Boo," Natasha said.
"Weed," Jen said.
"'ota," Michael A. said.
"Ganja," Jack said.
"A la Taj," Taj said.
"Grass," said Abilene.
"Gotcha," said Two Moons, nodding. "I call it 'God bud.'"

chapter fifteen

A happy Jack rushed into his and Jen's bedroom just as an exiting Natasha was saying to Jen, "I'm late and I'm dealing with it, okay?" Then she was gone and Jack said:

"I didn't mean to interrupt your girl talk, hon. I'm just stoked 'cause I aced my paper for Dr. Malof."

"It wasn't girl talk. It was women's stuff." Then, not giving it much, Jen said, "That's wonderful about your Malof paper, Jack. I didn't do as well on mine."

. . .

Fall's first norther was upon them, so Two Moons and Michael A. were up in the Crow's Nest flying the Purple Crab kite. Down in his room Taj was beside his gas heater and in a deep reverie in which he was recalling a time with his father. Often, when peeved at Taj, his father would say "Oh, go fly a kite" and one day the smart aleck in Taj had said, "May we?" That day came during Taj's first norther in Austin, a dark and cloudy Sunday in 1953. Father and son were in the middle of the median of what was then East Avenue but would soon become Austin's Berlin wall—Interstate 35—so as to separate the east side's blacks and browns from the whites on the west side.

From a length of string, two slender tree branches and the Sunday funny papers Taj's father had assembled a kite. It was flying high in the norther when Taj's dad left saying, "You're on your own."

So Taj lay on his back watching that funny-paper kite fly high in the sky. A patch of dark blue clouds came yet some sunlight still poured through and it looked like a waterfall to Taj who became so lost in this masterpiece by Mother Nature that when lightning streaks came he pretended that it was he who was shooting them through the sky. Taj came out of his reverie when Two Moons said to Michael A. up in the Crow's Nest:

"Can I get a tangerine tree so I can have tangerine dreams?" Next she said, "Chambawamba, am I peakin'. The Purple Crab kite has turned into a pterodactyl that's hovering over Cambridge Tower."

Aware they were stoned on the Texas Medicine that had been absorbed into their fingers earlier while filling double-aught capsules, Taj used a falsetto voice to say to them from down in his room, "Next time wear gloves when packing the gelatin caps."

"'ona?" said Michael A.

"Nooo," Taj said in his normal voice, "just a one-armed merry prankster."

. . .

It was 3 A.M. After band practice Taj, concerned about how Hannah and Boo Boo would handle their first norther, had gone up to the Crow's Nest. Now he was in his hamaca, Boo Boo in his hair and Hannah a curled up nest on his belly. Suddenly Hannah's ears pricked, her tail started to twitch from side to side and her eyes locked in on something. Taj saw her focus was on smoke rising from the second chimney. Seeing the smoke made him think back to another 3 A.M. back in August. It was after Que Tal's Gamma Sig gig and Taj, Jack and Michael A. were lugging band equipment out of the Gamma Sig house when a Gamma Sig pointed out how cool the 19th Street house looked with the UT Tower showing over the house's rooftop. When Taj had looked that way, he had seen a muted glow atop a chimney. To Jack it was Mona and he had said, "Well, I'll be goldurned. She's just sitting up there pretty as can be, ain't she?"

But now Taj wondered if, because of the perspective from the Gamma Sig house, what he and Jack had seen last August was not a muted glow but smoke.

"Where there is smoke there is fire," he said to Hannah. "But I do not think ghosts light fires."

Which was when Taj flinched from the unexpected sting of Hannah's claws digging into his belly and Boo Boo reacted to the flinch—*"Pwaaak!"*—by leaping from Taj's head to land talons-first on his shoulder. Taj then went back to his room … and found both animals waiting for him beside the gas heater.

"That makes twice you've done that," Taj said. "How are you doing it?"

. . .

After having readied the black-eyed peas with two weeks in the Hotpoint fridge, Bicycle Annie was showing the housemates how to shell this bounty from their garden: use a thumb to push the peas into a bowl then place the hulls in a brown paper bag that would be emptied onto the compost pile. While a listless one-armed Everyman watched, Natasha tried to distract him by pointing out the god's eye and dreamcatcher within a dreamcatcher she had hung in the kitchen window. She then began to sing "I Know You, Rider" and all of Que Tal joined in.

"There is nothing quite like five part harmony," Taj said afterwards.

. . .

Michael A. and Ryder moved the faded red couch out of the living room and onto the front porch. After setting it down next to the Fitty Six's naugahyde seat, Michael A. offered Ryder a $5 bill for his assistance.

"No thanx, I just sold some blood," Ryder said and ran off to chase some grackles out of the front yard. Right after this, Michael A. witnessed a radio-antenna-converted-to-a roach clip being telescoped out of Jack and Jen's bedroom window and heard Jack's voice saying:

"Carpe diem, Cuz."

"Ool," Michael A. said, knowing the radio antenna had been recycled from the Fitty Six. Next he took a drag off the roach in the attached alligator clip and said, "'exican?"

"No, it's Mugsy's Columbian. 'Ceebo' you called it."

"Mmmm"—nodding—"da 'uture."

. . .

Two Moons looked at the Volkswagen bus and said, "This is a smart investment, Jack."

"Time will tell," he said as he took from the bed of the Fitty Six the waterproof tarps used to cover the band equipment, a move that uncovered the cayuco *Analuz* and a box of Granpa Gage's whittled slingshot stocks.

"What a cool canoe and slingshot stocks," Two Moons said.

"The canoe is a Maya dugout made from a mahogany trunk and the slingshots are mesquite from the Chihuahua Desert,' Jack said. "My Grandfather Nacho gave me the canoe an' my Granpa Gage whittled the stocks."

"Your ancestors had powerful medicine."

"I agree. One was a Maya daykeeper who taught me I am another like yourself an' the other was a Texas Ranger who taught me to trust myself, be honest an' true."

"What's that carved into the bow of the cayuco?"

"*Analuz.*"

"Ah nah *loos?*"

"My mom's name. She was a jaguar warrior."

"How fortunate to have those three ancestors here with you."

"Yep. I'm always feelin' the lightning of each in my blood."

. . .

That evening at Jack's insistence Two Moons and Taj took *Analuz* for a spin on Town Lake. Both enjoyed the experience but for different reasons. Two Moons daydreamed she was in a Piegan canoe on a favorite stream back on The Rez while Taj was captivated by the waves rippling out from *Analuz's* wake.

"Wave power," Taj said.

"What's 'wave power?'"

"An idea still busy being born."

chapter sixteen

It was October 30, a Wednesday, and an hour ago the wire from Michael A.'s jaws had been removed. "Mooreburger and fries" were his first words and also his first solid food in four weeks. Now he was not a well man and an inner voice was saying "You're gonna urp, blow beets, spew great green gobs of greamy grimey gopher guts, projectile vomit all over the place." He had laid himself out on the faded red sofa when Natasha came into the living room. He noted no thunder-stomping of her combat boots, that her approach instead had body swish with some jiggle in her wiggle.

"Kudos," she said to Michael A. while holding up the cartoons with her caricature, the ones Michael A. had drawn after her post Wreck-of-the-Fitty Six taunt to be creative. "It's about time comics had empowered women."

Jen now came in humming a tune, only to stop short and say, "What's that smell?"

"Smoke," Natasha said. "It started right after the norther hit."

. . .

By now Jen's humming had caught on. Everybody in the house plus Ryder and Bicycle Annie was doing it and each had their own tune for Baby Maya.

Jen's was "Little Bitty One."

Jack's was "Spoonful."

Michael A.'s was "I Feel Free."

Taj's was "Only the Lonely."
Natasha's was "I Know You Rider."
Mrs. Medina's was "Stardust."
Two Moons' was "Who Do You Love."
Abilene's was Del Shannon's "Runaway."
Ryder's was "Take Five."
And Bicycle Annie's was Allen Sherman's "Hello Muddah, Hello Faddah."

. . .

October 31 was a Thursday with a Halloween Party at The Castle above 12th Street. Jen and Natasha had each just brushed their hair a hundred strokes and now they were primping in the mirror of the Ethan Allen boudoir, Jen on the vanity stool, Natasha behind her, Jen saying:
"Vanity is another stupid human trick."
"But it's also one of the keys to good health and can sometimes be a girl's best friend."
"I got a question for you," Jen said. "Are you'n this Oily George guy an item now?"
"Yep."
"My god, girl! What on *earth* for?"
"For reasons you'd never suspect." Then Natasha shrugged and said, "Maybe it's because politics make strange bedfellows. Or that I'm afraid of the dark and the dumb schmuck's too rich not to be afraid of me."

. . .

It was long after dark now and all the little devils, ghosts, ghouls, gremlins, goblins, vampires and werewolves had returned home to dig into their Halloween treats. Right now the real tricksters—there were nine of them packed into the VW bus—were turning off Lamar Boulevard onto 12th Street. The driver, Jack, was costumed as Herman Munster while Jen rode beside him as Mrs. Munster. Michael A. was, of course, the silver-tongued devil, his newly freed tongue glittering with sequins, his body in a red tuxedo with tails, his face made up with a goatee, pencil thin mustache and widow's peak. Taj was the one-armed man from TV's "The Fugitive" and Natasha was Natasha of the *Rocky and Bullwinkle Show*. Two Moons wore nothing but an extra large red T-shirt that said **HISTORY AIN'T CHANGED** and Abilene was dressed as *One Flew Over The Cuckoo's Nest's* Nurse Ratchett. Bicycle Annie, made up as a witch with a long droopy nose a la *The Wizard of Oz's* Wicked Witch of the West, gave some history, saying:

"The Castle was constructed in Gothic Revival style and is located at 1111 West 11th Street, a bluff overlooking downtown Austin and Shoal Creek which was Austin's first western boundary. Initially, The Castle was on 32 acres but that has shrunk to 1.2 acres. The Castle was built to be the Texas Military Institute and was completed around 1870. Its president was John Garland James and it was patterned after West Point though no professional soldiers were trained there. Its curriculum was proclaimed to be "non sectarian but religious." It closed in 1879 when President James resigned and took most of the faculty with him to a new state university that is now Texas A&M."

"Gig 'em, aggies," Michael A. said. "Parrrrteee."

"Right on, right on, right on," Natasha said.

"Hell yeah, let's party," Jack said. "Me'n Jen's been cooped up parentin' for so long we'd go to a buzzard stomp."

"I would most certainly *not* do that," said Jen.

Taj next began a rhythmic slap on his right thigh, all joining in, harmonizing:

"*Parrrrteee. Parrrrteee. Parrrrteee.*"

. . .

A good time was had by all. It was a gathering of the tribe, a get-together for the cabbages and kings, the freaks and hairies, dykes and fairies of Austin's In-Groovy-Head-Crowd. Amid black lights undulating, lava lamps bubbling and a psychedelic light show clouding the mota smoke the Light Fantastic was tripped, all mental gravity was cast off and everybody was tripping. Lucy was in her Sky and her Diamonds were sparkling. Kaleidoscope eyes were delightfully dilated as hippies danced with one arm swinging free while wiggling and giggling to

the Rhythm That Was Them. And their words worked weird wonders within winsome windows:
    "Like wowww, man, I am the octopus."
    "It ain't me, babe."
    "I am The Leg Man! I am The Leg Man!"
    "And I am the Electric Kool Aid Acid Test."
    "Ya know, darlin', I got a castle too. It's—"
    "Where? On your frontal lobe?"
    "Cool. Utterly supercalifragilisticexperhalitosis."
    "What's green'n red'n goes ninety miles an hour?"
    "What?"
    "A frog in a blender."
    "Onward through the frog."

chapter seventeen

It was Friday, November 1, the Day of the Dead and Michael A. and Ma planned to visit his father's grave in the state cemetery off Hancock Drive. But first Michael A. had to phone Uncle Tunoose down in the Big House. So he walked to the Student Union's bank of pay phones outside the Chuck Wagon, inserted the requested amount of coins and asked for Uncle Tunoose. What he was told was:

"Nobody here by that name."

Michael A. then said, "Tell him his nephew called" and the party at the other end's response was to say "He is no longer with us" and hung up.

Confused, Michael A. went home. There he learned from Two Moons—rushing out the door for her math class—that Ma had just gone with the church ladies to the cemetery. So he went out to the front porch with his Slinky and the globe of the world from Big John's House of Crap. He spun the globe then stopped the spinning with his index finger and saw that he had landed on Spain. Next he sent his Slinky down the oak plank steps daydreaming of Delilah, Castle Hostel and his time as Parc Guell's Salamander blues singer. Lastly, he got down on his belly on the faded red couch and let his godawful ugly toes dangle over the couch's edge. Soon he was daydreaming he was aboard the *Zak Be* as the 42' ketch rode anchor over Itzamal Reef above the Octopus's Garden. In his reverie he was stretched out in a Maya blue matrimonial-size hamaca shaded by a tarp strung between the main mast and forestay. Tied to the stern rail was a kite adorned with the glyph for the Maya creator god called Not Right Now and as it flew high in the sky Michael A. dreamt a dream full of feelings. He dreamt of his father the military man so often absent in his son's life and how Captain Medina was now gone forever, had said goodbye to the sky. Though their relationship as father and son had often been restrained, there had always been respect. The captain had been in three wars but all he had ever said about them was "They got a little of my blood and I got some of theirs." Michael A. now opened one eye to see through a one-eyed squint a column of ants marching between the latest issue of *The Rag* and *The Ranger*, the latter the University's student humor magazine. He was on the verge of dozing off when he heard footsteps. Squinting again, he saw government shoes and assumed it was the postman. But then he heard an eerily familiar voice say:

"Go to the ants, thou sluggard. Consider their ways."

One squint at the speaker and a goggle-eyed Michael A. said, "Uncle Tunoose? Is that really you?"

"In the flesh, nephew, and wearing government shoes and a suit of clothes with $5 in the pocket. Which is how the Texas Prison System releases you back into the general population."

"Que tal, y'all," another voice said.

"Ohhh, heyyy, look, it's Rosko," Michael A. said to the Elf of Velvet Fortune standing at the top of the porch steps and holding a colorful Maya rucksack. "Bis be, Rosko. The more the merrier. Ha ha—very clever that 'Que tal, y'all.' Yeah, that's a good one for this part of the planet."

"When in Rome…," said Rosko and dropped the rucksack to plop down and spin the globe of the world then stop it with his finger. He was shirtless and tan and wore a pair of white linen slacks with chanclas on his sockless feet. Though still bald as a cue ball, his youthful smile and the twinkle in his eye made him seem spry, wry and sly, very sly as he took from his rucksack a Big Chief tablet and began to scribble doodle.

Michael A. said to Uncle Tunoose who, unlike Rosko, was not showing even a speck of a smile, "So, uh, what was it that got you sprung from the Big House? Good behavior? You, uh, didn't escape, did you?"

"I tolja I was workin' on gettin' sprung. How's the jaw?"

"They just took the wire off. It'll take a while to get back to normal again."

"Tell me about it. Rejoining the general population ain't gonna be no piece of cake neither."

"You look good," Michael A. said, lying a little.

"It ain't my looks that hurt."

"But how come—" Stopping when his uncle held up his hand to say:

"The 'how come,' nephew, is State's Evidence. Since dead men tell no tales, I turned Nacho in after he croaked. Nacho was better than a brother but—"

"Oh, *si, si*," said Rosko, not looking up from his Big Chief tablet, "mucho *mejor* than a brother."

"But life is for the living," said Uncle Tunoose.

"It ain't Code of the West to rat out a pal, Uncle. You did a dirty deed. It was plumb pitiful what you did."

"Sez who? My smart aleck nephew what's always poppin' off?"

"Michael A. has a point," Rosko said.

"Nacho don't mind," Uncle Tunoose said. "What's done is done, end of story." When Michael A. said nothing, he said, "I could flop down at the Alamo Hotel like I used to but I was kinda hoping 200 West 19th Street would be the Big House for me now. I been locked up so long that just flopping out here on the porch'd be okay. By the way, I sleep in the raw—is that against the rules?"

Rosko said, "You walk out of the house and you see someone naked and you say 'Who is that man?'"

"We no longer got any rules so raw's okay," Michael A. said. "An' you're welcome to crash here too, Rosko. Ma will be happy to see you."

"Muchas gracias, Michael A. I very much look forward to seeing my dear friend Maisie as well as meeting your fellow transcendent beings in Que Tal. There are hamacas on the roof, yes?"

"Yep. Feel free to crash in any of 'em."

"And Miss Mona? I shall see her on the roof, yes?"

"Maybe. She's been spotted up there."

Rosko made some quick pen strokes on his scribble doodle then presented it to Michael A. saying, "Please accept this as my gratitude for the hamaca."

The drawing impressed Michael A. but not Uncle Tunoose. Peering over his nephew's shoulder, he said, "That Don Quixote dude a*gain?*"

"Si, and his windmill *tambien*," Rosko said. "Though most minds have mountains, mine has windmills."

. . .

That evening Sofia came out onto the front porch with Baby Maya in her arms. She walked over to where Tunoose sat in Granpa Gage's bentwood rocker, handed him the infant and said:

"Meet your daughter, Miss Maya Karma Gage."

With Baby Maya reaching for his chin, a befuddled Tunoose said, "Does anyone else know she's mine?"

"No one."

"Can you keep it a secret?"

"All my life I've kept men's secrets—my father's, Nacho's, my husband's, my son's, yours."

Tunoose said, "I have agreed with myself that it's best she never knows who I am." Then he lay his hand on Maya and said to his sister, "Like my man on the scene says, 'Life's a trip.' Nacho's daughter Chanil falls in love with pig-ignorant me, we marry and Nacho becomes my father-in-law. Then his son rats me out, I get sent to the Big House, Nacho becomes grandfather to this child and I am widowed. The birth of a child is not always a joyous event."

"Nobody gets to you like—"

"Misery and pain then more misery and pain."

"Maya is loved and in good hands."

"Yes, and she'll grow up strong and well adjusted. But I shall see none of it."

"What do you mean?"

"Sofia, I'm going home."

"Tunoose, you know you can't go back to Lebanon."

"I don't want to go back. What I'm saying is my time is near, that with every breath I'm closer to death."

"Stop it, Tunoose, you're not old enough to die."

"Death doesn't discriminate against age. Last night I swallowed a tooth in my sleep and you know what they say that means back in the old country."

"Are you in pain?"

"Just like a woman. Tell 'em where you're going an' when ya come back they wanta know where ya been."

"Have you seen a doctor?"

"Pecker checkers are no good to me now. I'm done for. I just hope I got enough time to put my affairs in order."

"You're absolutely sure about this?"

"The State of Texas is. It's why I got sprung. Life is for the living an' death is for everybody … hell, life itself is a death sentence."

This was when Sofi reached over to give Maya a loving caress and say, "Long live life."

chapter eighteen

Not unlike a bee or a hummingbird, Rosko was a vibrant life force, one who brought nectar and ambrosia to not only the 19th Street house but all he met. When it was decided that Que Tal would go wild with the money in the three lock box, Rosko became Mr. Designated Spender with Maisie for an accomplice. On their first foray they went to Academy Surplus across from Hancock Center on Interstate 35 and bought fifty pairs of longjohn underwear and farmer john overalls. Next Rosko and Maisie went to La Vaca Lana. From Mayapan they bought large amounts of tortillas, bread and jars of Yucatecan honey. At Oedibles they bought out the Plato Azul Special. From Viva Zapatas they scored dozens of pairs of chanclas and Piegan moccasins. From Hoochie Mamas they purchased Jen and Cool Breeze generic T-shirts plus wool blankets Jack that had ordered from Aunt Asilee. Then Mr. Designated Spender and Maisie put the whole haul in the pink Caddy and gave it away at the Town Lake K.O.A.

Mr. Designated Spender also donated to the United Farm Workers Union, the Democratic Party and Free Clinic.

And for some reason he bought a hundred cases of Swiss chocolate.

. . .

The coast was clear and all through the house nary a housemate could be found. Mr. Designated Spender, Maisie, Abilene and Baby Maya were on another Town Lake K.O.A. run. Taj was introducing Two Moons to Tex Mex at Matt's El Rancho Restaurant at 302

East First Street. Ryder was gone for the day, Natasha was working at the library and Michael A. and Uncle Tunoose—now a dead ringer in his overalls and long johns for Walter Brennan as "The Real McCoys" Granpa McCoy—had gone to Hyde Park Recreation to shoot pool. Therefore, Jack and Jen had time alone and when Jen heard their bedroom door close then saw Jack leaning against it wearing a generic T-shirt that said *Coming Soon*, she knew that something was up. In fact, she had been counting on it, her only article of clothing a T-shirt saying *For Jack Only*.

"Whatcha readin'?" he said with that certain look on his face.

"Gore Vidal's latest, *Myra Breckinridge*," she said with a coy grin. "I got it as soon as it hit the New Books shelf at the library."

"Michael A. says Raquel Welch has the title role in the movie an' UT's very own Farrah Fawcett'll be in it too."

They then made eyes at each other until Jen said, "What ya got in mind, Jaaack? Another game of Monopoly?"

"Nawww. But I am a rich 'un so ya oughta marry me."

"But, Ben Jack Gage"—playing innocent—"you know little ol' me is already engaged to Like the Nite."

Jack said, "And does Walks In Beauty think she's snagged herself a good'ern?"

"Time will tell, mister." Batting her sapphire eyes before saying, "How's your hip?"

"Tolerable."

Smiling slyly, she said, "Does Cowboy have a hitch in his git-along too?"

"No, ma'am. He's as pert as a ruttin' buck."

"Think he'd be up for gettin' rode hard'n put up wet?'

"Yesss, maaam."

Jen winked and said, "Jack be nimble, Jack be quick. Jaaack, love me wild."

"Yes'um." Then tore off his *Coming Soon* T-shirt.

"You're on, mister" and shed her *For Jack Only* top.

. . .

The pool parlor dude's return to Hyde Park Recreation was akin to a king's triumphant return from exile. The regulars lined up and paid their respects. They bowed their heads and shook his hand. One even kissed that hand. A big deal was made of reuniting Tunoose with his personal cue stick. No one said a word about his government shoes.

One guy, though, the heir apparent now demoted back to being just another soldier, made a point of saying, "I ain't gonna kiss his hand or any other part of him."

"Me neither," Michael A. said, trying to sound tough before walking over to his uncle with some bad news.

"Is this is a $1000 bill you're giving me?" Uncle Tunoose said with a scowl.

"Yeah. See, it's got Grover Cleveland on it. I also got a $500 bill with William McKinley on it. Thought you might like 'em for souvenirs."

"You let somebody stick you with these turkeys? Ya can't take 'em to a bank. Can't spend 'em neither. Souvenirs is all they're good for."

"Yeah. 'No witnesses, no crime,' 'conspicuous consumption' an' all like that. Ya think Mr. Designated Spender could pass 'em?"

"That's our only hope," said Uncle Tunoose. "Rosko's the closest thing we got to a talisman of the leisure class."

chapter nineteen

Jack was outside his and Jen's bedroom getting his essay paper out of his Maya rucksack when he heard Natasha inside saying, "The best part's the dumb schmuck's a real credit to his gender 'cause he thinks it's his." Then she rushed past Jack as she left the bedroom.

"Guess what," Jack said to Jen, showing her his essay.

"What?" Not looking at him from down on the floor.

"I got an 'A' from Dr. Ayres."

"That's wonderful, dear. I didn't do so well." Jen was on the floor beside the waterbed, her face showing strain because she was doing an exercise routine. "I tried something new today," she said as Jack bent over the waterbed to begin changing Baby Maya's diaper. "I went online with a Harvard professor at the computer center."

"You did *whut* with this guy?"

"I used a computer"—face showing strain—" to talk to a Harvard professor."

Jack lay Maya down on a clean diaper spread out on the bed and said, "Ya lost me, hon. What's 'online' mean?"

"It means 'computer to computer.'" Pausing to strain. "I saw and heard a lecture 2000 miles away. I even asked a question."

Due to the safety pins in his mouth, Jack just grunted.

"It's the future," Jen said, straining. "Someday we'll all be linked up to computers. They'll pay the bills, show us the movies, the news, they'll be the library."

"Bulll." Jack said and finished pinning Maya's diaper as Jen got off the floor to lie down beside their daughter. After a deep breath, she said:

"It's time for her nap."

Lying down next to them, Maya in between them, Jack said, "Hon? What was all the straining for?"

"It's part of the Kegel exercise."

"Whut's it spose to do?"

"It contracts and relaxes the pubococcygeus muscles in my pelvis and this improves the muscle tone of my pelvic floor. It's good for vaginal prolapse and preventing uterine prolapse."

"Oh. Women's stuff."

"Not entirely. Kegeling can also reduce urinary incontinence in men as well as premature ejaculatory occurrences."

"Shhh, hon. You're disturbing the baby."

Jen just grinned. She knew full well it was not Maya she was disturbing.

. . .

Michael A. was saying to Bicycle Annie, "When will the beans in the garden be ready to harvest?"

"Somebody already harvested 'em."

"Who? The goats?"

"I doubt it. They're always tethered."

"Caca pasa, chachalaca?"

"Maybe." Shrug. "Maybe not."

Michael A. frowned and said, "Let's go for a spin, Annie. It's high time we got our guard back up to snuff around here."

. . .

They took the pink Caddy to Town Lake Animal Shelter. Once there they browsed, they made eye contact, they spoke doggie terms of endearment through the cage doors. Finally, Michael A. said:

"What about these two?"

"I expect they'll do," Annie said, "once they're past the 'cute puppie' stage an' can actually *guard* something."

"Then I hereby christen these two dawgs 'Bewiled'n Beepley'.

. . .

They were just two more mutts from the Austin Animal Shelter. There was no garbage they would not forage, no tree Bewiled would not hike a leg on or that Beepley would squat on. There were also no shoes, boots, chanclas or moccasins they would not chew on. There was only one pair of ankles they would bite, though, and, consequently and pair by pair, they chewed up Michael A.'s white Converse tennies. And all too many mornings did a fogbound Mr. Dynamic Tension arise from the faded red couch thinking he was stepping into a shoe only to curse at the stinky-gooey discovery that his bare foot was in a pile of poo or a pool of pee. And always next could be heard a snickering in the front bedroom followed by Jack saying:

"Dogs run free, Michael A. Dogs run free."

. . .

"A little to the right and I'll really feel it."

"There?" Jack said.

"More, more … there. Right *there!*"

"Hush up, Jen, or you'll wake the baby."

"I bet Michael A. gets a room at the Sheraton Crest."

"Nawww, he goes up to the Crow's Nest."

"He does it in a hamaca? How's that work?"

"Very carefully." Stretching himself out beside her. "Doncha remember us doin' it in Palenque?"

"Of course I do."

"Then hush up an' save a horse."

"Say what?"

"Ride a Cowboy."

Jen grinned, moved atop him and said, "Gotcha covered."

. . .

Though the door was closed to his bedroom, Jack came barging in just as Jen, seated beside Natasha on the water bed and holding her hand, was saying:

"Daphne says there's a doctor in Carrollton who'll do it."

"Oops, sorry," Jack said, embarrassed, and was turning to leave when Natasha pulled her hand away from Jen's, got to her feet and said:

"We're done." Then she rushed out of the room.

"Sorry I busted up your women's stuff talk, Jen," Jack said. "I just wanted you to know I got an 'A' on my Shakespeare paper."

"That's wonderful, Jack. I only got a 'C.'"

. . .

Michael A. kissed his paperback copy of Joseph Heller's *Catch-22* and said to it, "Milo Minderbinder, you are a man after my own heart. Yep, you'n me're two peas in a pod. We both got vision'n imagination so we're goin' for it. Gettin' my Triumph back'll make me whole again. One world, one planet. Oh hell yeah, am I gonna shoot some lightning through the sky." Then he rubbed his hands together in sinister fashion and took the keys from Jen who then said to Jack standing next to her:

"After the Wreck of the Fitty Six I just couldn't see Baby Maya riding papoose style."

"Nobody tells me nothin' 'til it's a done deal," Jack said. But he was smiling because he was glad Jen no longer was driving the Triumph 650.

. . .

So there he was again: throwing his leg over her, kick-starting her on the third try, about to take her for a spin, go cruisin' for burgers on what was once more his burgundy Triumph 650 motorcycle. For his first spin he would do what he had promised himself back on October 1: see his former homes in Austin. 1019 Elba Place was off 45th Street and was up on concrete blocks with a real estate agent's sign nailed to a front porch post. Nearby was a sign put up by the Texas Highway Department saying this site would soon be part of Mopac Expressway.

Next Michael A. headed for the last house in Austin in which he had lived, a duplex at 2801-B Hemphill Park. It amused him to see it was full of hippies.

He then rode the Triumph to the first house he had called home. On East Seventh he made a left then a right on Canadian Street. After a left turn onto Second and a Half Street he was there. 1174 East Second and a Half Street held his earliest memories, where he had first lamented being an only child, had wished for a sibling to pester. It was also where he had been dubbed 'Michael A.' so folks could distinguish between him and his father. Michael A., however, had wanted to be called "Snafu," his dad having told him it was an army term meaning "situation normal—all flubbed up." 1174 East Second and a Half was also where Michael A. had his first father-son talk the day his dad came back from the Korean War. It was on the back porch step and the seven-year-old did not understand anything other than that they were selling the house and moving to Elba Street because of President Eisenhower's Operation Wetback. His dad's first advice for his son had come on that day: "Buy land 'cause they're not making any more." His dad had also mentioned something about large numbers of people living together: "The function of cities and towns is social interaction so we're gonna move to North Austin 'cause there's too many illegals here in this part of town and I don't want to risk you and your mom getting caught up in Operation Wetback." When Michael A. asked "What was the war like?" his dad had said:

"They got a little of my blood and I got a little of theirs."

. . .

Michael A. rode into the driveway of the 19th Street house to find Two Moons by her tipi and Ryder brushing Nachita, Nubia and Monita. Though Two Moons rushed over to show Michael A. the new Thirteen Floor Elevators album "Easter Everywhere" and Big Brother and the Holding Company's new album "Cheap Thrills," he initially gave them short shrift and instead said:

"How come Ryder's always tending to your goats?"

"Because, silly, they're *his* goats."

"When did they become his?"

"When they were born. Ryder's also a Piegan. He had to leave the goats behind when he went into the Navy."

"He was in the Navy, huh?"

"Uh huh. He was on the *USS Pueblo* and the *Liberty*."

"Really? The *Pueblo*?"

"And the *Liberty*."

"Never heard of it."

"You will. It and My Lai."

chapter twenty

On Saturday morning, November 2, Ryder set up a big brass bed for Uncle Tunoose on the east end of the front porch. Ryder then added some privacy by nailing 4X8' lattices to the east and south sides of the porch. Later, Taj came out to the porch because he heard a saxophone playing a blue serenade. It was Ryder playing the sax he had found in the attic. On the big brass bed Tunoose was struggling to put on his government shoes. When Ryder stopped playing, Taj said:

"You are very good, Ryder."

Tunoose said, "He's been sittin' in with Wet Willie'n Merle at The Lounge. He's learnin' to be a jeweler too. We need a jeweler." Tunoose then said to Ryder, "How's life at 6th an' Guadalupe?"

"The Alamo Hotel suits me fine, sir."

"Is LBJ's brother still livin' there?"

"Yessir, but that don't bother me none."

"Thanks for gettin' me this big brass bed. I might just die in it."

"We should move it inside during cold weather, sir."

"Maybe we will, but thanks to a shirttail relative I just did a stretch in the cooler so I figure I can handle the cold." Then to Taj, he said, "I guess all y'all're curious about Ryder, so I'll fill you in an' you can pass it along to the others. Ya see Nacho bought this house for reasons that, well, didn't pan out. Next it was a music academy what went belly up so it became my stash house."

"For Slinkys, Hula Hoops, Frisbees," said Taj, nodding.

"And sometimes for boo, some Senor Fuego tequila." Tunoose then paused to grin before saying, "But then Nacho got it in his head that you kids should move in."

"Good old Nacho," Taj said.

"The man wasn't no angel. But I gotta say it's turned out well. So far anyway."

"I agree," Taj said. "Que Tal and Xutan Partners are flourishing as are Purple People Eater and La Vaca Lana."

Tunoose winked and said, "An' leave us not forget them bees an' hummingbirds."

"Be assured, sir, that they shall not be forgotten."

"The only downer," said Tunoose, "has been the shirttail relative that was my original man on the scene. When I kicked him out so Que Tal could move in, he finked an' got me sent to the Big House. Cool Breeze became my man on the scene but then he kicked the bucket. Now Ryder's my man on the scene. You savvy?"

"'Man on the scene' is an unusual job description," Taj said. Turning to Ryder, he said, "What is your interpretation?"

"I keep an eye out plus I poke around for wampum."

Seeing that Taj was baffled by "wampum," Tunoose said, "Because this house was built in the 1840s, it seems to me there oughta be something here what's worth pokin' around for."

"Ahhh, wampum," Taj said, thinking of the three lock box he had found in the attic. "What have you found so far, Ryder?"

"So far just this big brass bed in the root cellar beneath the back porch. I think somebody's been floppin' down there." Then, grinning, he said, "I also found what makes that mystery bell sound we've all heard. It's a mouse living in the front door's ringer."

"Very good," Taj said with a smile. "But let us not mention this mouse to Jen. She has a profound aversion to infestation."

. . .

What Goes Bump In The Night was miffed about losing the big brass bed to Tunoose since it meant that, yet again, he would have to come up with a new place to flop. His only option was to move into the hidey-hole.

And, man oh man, did he hate having to do that.

. . .

It was Sunday afternoon, November 3 and Rosko and Maisie were wading in the water on Town Lake's north shore. Nearby Bicycle Annie, Michael A. and Uncle Tunoose—his daughter asleep in his lap—sat in the shade of the Montopolis Bridge. The men were drinking Pearl longnecks and cane pole fishing and Bicycle Annie was saying to them:

"The Montopolis Bridge was completed in 1938 after the devastating flood of June 15, 1935. It consists of five 200-foot Parker trusses and fifty-two-foot steel I-beams set on concrete abutments."

"I've been lucky in this spot," Uncle Tunoose said.

"You've been bringin' me to this spot for as long as I can remember an' I never caught nothin' but a cold," said Michael A. "Or did you mean you got lucky with a gal here?"

"At this time of my life, nephew, 'got lucky' means I made it to the can on time."

Michael A. now heard his Ma laugh and this made him frown and say, "That Rosko is a real rascal."

"The more I know the less I understand," his uncle said. "Can't you see how happy your mother is?"

"Rosko's old enough to be her grandfather."

"It's not the age but the moment, nephew."

Bicycle Annie snickered and said. "That old man has your mother acting like a young girl again. She told me she's gonna join the Metrecal for Lunch Bunch so she can lose weight."

Michael A. said, "I'm not so sure Rosko's really who he says he is."

Tunoose scowled. "At least you got guts to go with your gall. Like I told you, me'n Nacho've known Rosko since the war. He's a tough old bird with a hard bark on him but he's always been as good as gold. He owns nothing yet he's got everything." Uncle Tunoose then grew quiet and seemed to revel in the tranquil scene around him. After a sigh, he said, "A man could grow figs here." Next he said to Michael A., "I heard about Cool Breeze's big sendoff. Ya know how I want it for the Great Beyond, right?"

"Yep. You'll be recyclin' fo'ever'n ever' in the Gulf Stream. I, however, want my ashes put in an hour glass."

"What in the world for?"

"'Cause that way I'll be working fo'ever'n ever."

. . .

The handbills they printed on Michael A.'s little printing press called it "Radio Free Austin." But among themselves they called it "Radio Reefer." Its transmitter—with 'Kilroy was here' etched on it—used the test frequency 100.1. It had a range of one mile and was hidden in a sculpture by Ryder that he called "Hideosity": the bed of the Fitty Six serving as the base for the Kawasaki's melted remains. Radio Reefer was broadcast from the 19th Street house's living room. A second Teac reel to reel was bought and when it was not playing pre-recorded music, Reefer's disc jockeys were Jen, Jack, Taj, Natasha, Michael A. and Wet Willie whose nom du aires were Dusty Street, Junior, Everyman, Dinahmite, Freewheelin and Wet Willie. Whenever Ryder and Maisie spinned platters, they were just Ryder and Maisie, Ryder spinning saxophone records, Maisie playing Little Jimmy Valentine and other 1940s music. Radio Reefer debuted November 4, 1968, with Que Tal's version of Cream's "I Feel Free."

Radio Reefer did not take long to catch on. Not only did the Gamma Sigs perpetually blast it out of their frat house and cars but Bicycle Annie said she heard it all over campus.

. . .

Ryder came out onto the front porch and said to Tunoose, Taj and Michael A., "Wait'll ya hear this. I was pokin' around outside the west wall and behind some vines I find the chimney for the hidden living room fireplace. I figure this is a good spot to place the six-foot copper rod needed to ground Radio Reefer's antenna. So I drive the rod down into the soil, but I hit air. And when I dig around it looks like the chimney goes down as far as Songcatcher. I go inside the house, go down to Songcatcher. I see a loose floorboard, so I pry it up and see more chimney. An when I pound the copper rod down along the chimney, guess what? I hit air again."

"This is cave country," Michael A. said, "so I guess there's a cave there."

Joking, Taj said, "Or perhaps it is Mona's deep dark hole."

"Whatever it is," said Uncle Tunoose, "I see it as a hidey-hole."

. . .

Michael A. was in the garage loading diapers into the Maytag washer. With Baby Maya in her crib beside him he was humming "I Feel Free" except for when he would hold up a diaper, sigh and say, "Author! Author!" or "Tinkle, tinkle, little star." He was uttering the latter when Jack showed up, the new puppies, Bewiled and Beepley nipping at their heels.

"These ain't no goldurn dogs, Cuz. They're just puppies an' what we need is guard dogs."

"Guard goats ain't enough?"

"Nope. There's somethin' in the house."

"You think so too, huh?"

"Yep," Jack said. "Mona or not, we ain't alone in there, Cuz."

chapter twenty one

Tuesday, November 5, was election day and Michael A., Jack and Natasha were away voting for the first time. On the east side of the 19th Street house autumn was in full bloom and her leaves were falling on Jen and Hannah. There, beside Wiley and Beep Beep's favorite oak tree, Hannah lay on her back getting some sun while Jen tidied up her dogs' graves and also where Taj's arm was buried. She was spreading the pebbles she had gathered alongside the trail to Cochise's Stronghold when Taj walked up.

"Why did you name her Hannah, Taj?"

"It was my mother's name."

"Who are Hannah's four sisters named for?"

"My own sisters."

"Oh. You miss your family, huh?"

"Yes. They are gone forever. *Desaparecidos*."

"What do you mean they're 'disappeareds?'"

Taj seemed to struggle before saying, "My father gave sanctuary to a rebel. Acting out of revenge, *el presidente* made my mother and sisters disappear. I was so traumatized when I learned this that I became mute."

"Wow. No closure." Jen then sighed and said, "I have a letter from my father I cannot bring myself to read."

Taj said, "Do you realize that only Michael A. among us has a parent?"

"Que Tal is our family."

"Of which I am a member because Rosko knew Uncle Tunoose a long time ago."

"I think there's more to it than that," Jen said. Then she said, "Have you ever wondered how Rosko and Tunoose and Nacho got together?"

Taj shrugged and said, "Quien sabe?" As Hannah now sat up on her haunches and started to wash her face, he said, "Do you know how Hannah gets in the house?"

"It's not this oak tree?"

"The oak tree is how she gets up to the Crow's nest. I don't know how she gets inside the house."

"Hmmm, I wonder if that's how Boo Boo keeps showing up in my bedroom when its door is closed."

. . .

On November 5 Richard M. Nixon became the 37th president-elect of the United States of America, getting 43.4 percent of the vote to Humphrey's 42.7. That night at Batts Auditorium Purple People Eater Productions showed Charlie Chaplin's *The Little Dictator*. The profit was $612 but triple that would be reported.

On November 8 the church-door-turned-dining-room table became a buffet as Rosko made paella for eleven. Steve Miller and New Atlantis played the Vulcan Gas Company to which the VW bus transported all eleven buffet-goers.

On November 12 as a sly tribute to Uncle Tunoose Purple People Eater Productions showed *The Lion In Winter* starring Katherine Hepburn and Peter O'Toole. The take was $714 but triple that would be reported. Uncle Tunoose's reaction to the tribute was "Awww, phooey."

On November 13 Natasha and her SDS comrades were on the Student Union patio to hear Arbor Vitae and watch Curtain Club Theater protesting conditions for students and employees in the Chuck Wagon.

November 14 was National Turn In Your Draft Card Day. Meanwhile, Texas Pacific and Blues Bag played a Bail Bond Benefit at the Vulcan.

Since the only means of buying tickets was at the door, Mr. Designated Spender laid out enough moolah for a full house.

On November 15 Freddie King and Johnny Winter played the Vulcan and the VW bus set a new passenger record when Wet Willie rode on the roof.

. . .

It was Sunday morning, November 17. Across the street a Gamma Sig radio playing Radio Reefer playing Manfred Mann's "Mighty Quinn" awoke Michael A. To his considerable consternation and amazement he discovered he had been in repose atop the black church-door-turned-dining-room-table wearing only a pair of white athletic socks and his army green boxer shorts. His head hurt, his feet stank—particularly his ungodly ugly toes—and his neck had a crick in it. The last he could recall of the evening before was watching *A Night To Remember,* the flick about an iceberg's 1912 sinking of the *Titanic* that claimed more than a thousand lives. Among the dead was the ship's entire band who had played their instruments right up until the end.

"And the band played on," Michael A. said.

Michael A. next realized that he was home alone. Unbeknownst to him, Ma and Uncle Tunoose had connived Jack and Jen into taking Baby Maya to church for her christening and Natasha and Taj were at a revolutionary powwow at 609 West 23rd Street, office of *The Rag.* At first Michael A. was alarmed, but then decided to embrace his situation. To Thelma and Barney Lou in their fish bowl he said, "Alas, alack, no one here but we three an' your family. Shall we dance and frolic? Mayhaps be madcap with ferocity and denial?" This was when a low noise came from the living room, a scratching in the wall behind the faded red couch. So Michael A. bowed politely toward that low noise and said, "Plus Mona of course, can't omit ol' Mona." Nonplussed, he sashayed around the church-door-turned-dining-room-table saying, "The god of hellfire has 200 West 19th Street all to himself! Onward through the fog!" He then bolted from the dining room into the living room to turn to his left, striking a skater's pose as his momentum glided him over the slick oak floor into the entryway. He was about to go through the screen door onto the front porch to pick up the Sunday edition of the *Austin American Statesman* when he saw Hannah. Her gaze was fixed on the front door, more specifically on its old timey ringer where, according to Ryder, a mouse lived. In that moment the mouse stuck his head out of the ringer and saw Hannah, so the mouse ducked back inside the ringer which then rang. Michael A. grinned and said:

"Top that, Mona."

And of course Mona did.

. . .

On Monday, November 18, at the end of a particularly rousing "Crossroads" there came a sound in the north wall of Songcatcher Studio.

"Maybe it's the plumbing," Natasha said.

"I think not since we are all here," Taj said.

"It could be air in the pipes," Jack said.

"It could also be infestation," Jen said.

Meanwhile, in the darkness below What Goes Bump In The Night was miffed at himself for being such a klutz.

. . .

On November 19 the United Nations General Assembly voted 58 to 44 to reject a resolution to seat Communist China.

. . .

The night of November 21 the VW bus took Que Tal, Uncle Tunoose, Rosko, Abilene and Two Moons the seventy miles down Interstate 35 to San Antonio. At the Theatre For The Performing Arts at the Hemisphere Arena performing were Big Brother and the Holding Company, Johnny Winter and Shiva's Headband. Backstage, Pearl took one look at the one-armed Taj and said:

"What the heck happened to you?"

"Caca pasa, chachalaca. A motorcycle accident. I was slow on the uptake. I had no stage presence."

"Wow. Are ya keeping busy?"

"As busy as a one-armed paper hanger in a vacuum."

"Thatta boy."

Shortly thereafter, Janis Joplin, having fulfilled her contractual obligation, left Big Brother.

. . .

It was Friday morning 4 A.M., November 22, when Que Tal arrived back in Austin from San Antonio. Before heading home they stopped for 30-cents-a-dozen-day-old donuts at Mrs. Johnson's Bakery on Airport Boulevard. They were digging into these delights while seated around the church-door-turned-dining room table when Taj brought in the newspaper. Upon learning that it had been five years since the assassination of John F. Kennedy in Dallas, all of Que Tal went mum until Jen said:

"That morning Jolinda Biggs and I were outside Fort Worth's Hotel Texas when the President came out and I guess, because of the rain and cold, said to the crowd, 'There are no faint hearts in Fort Worth.' I'll never forget it. The man's charisma totally blew me away."

"I heard about it in Fred Henry's algebra class," said Michael A. "Me'n Charlie Thompson were swappin' lies in the back row. I wanted to join the Peace Corps that day but I was too young."

Jack said, "I was at football practice working through the pain of being blindsided by Scooter Culero when Coach told us."

Taj said, "I was in Tabriz, Iran. A mullah was shouting from a minaret, "Praise Allah for slaying Satan's spawn! Praise Allah for dispatching Satan's offal!"

Natasha said, "I was at 24th and Guadalupe singing "Jesus Wants Me For A Sun Beam."

Rosko said, "Princess Grace and I were at the casino in Monaco talking about how every creation is first an act of destruction."

Uncle Tunoose said, "I was at Hyde Park Rec shootin' pool while waitin' on a load of Frisbees."

Two Moons said, "There was a blizzard, so we had to stay in the tipi and didn't find out until the next day."

Abilene said, "I was at recess. They let us go home."

. . .

On the evening of November 22 Mance Lipscomb played the Vulcan Gas Company. When the old sharecropper was done with his set, an elated Uncle Tunoose told everybody around him, "Now I can leave this world."

. . .

On November 27 Jack put down a letter from Aunt Asilee. For a long moment he tapped his cane on a front porch oak plank. Finally, he said to Michael A., "I ain't gonna complain about my luck. At least not since Scooter Culero got himself blown up in Vietnam."

"I'm awful sorry to hear that, Jack."

"He ain't dead. But he's all stove up an' hooked on pain killers."

chapter twenty two

November 28 was Thanksgiving Day. When Michael A. asked Uncle Tunoose what he wanted for dinner, the old man said, "Figs, pickled pig's knuckles an' pecan pie'd be fine'n dandy." He then spent the afternoon listening to Radio KTBC broadcast the Texas Longhorns defeating the Texas A&M Aggies in Memorial Stadium a few blocks away. By late afternoon the old man's glass of Senor Fuego tequila was empty but he had barely touched his figs, pickled pig's knuckles and pecan pie. Everyone else was sitting near Uncle Tunoose's big brass bed and shelling pecans collected from Mrs. Smalley's trees after Jack and Ryder had used Tunoose and Michael A.'s fishing poles to knock them loose. The bounty had then been scooped into Minimax brown paper bags by Jen, Natasha, Abilene and Two Moons.

Eventually, Uncle Tunoose set aside his glass to prop himself up in his big brass bed. Jen placed Baby Maya in the crook of his left arm and both were soon surrounded by Boo Boo, Hannah and Hannah's visiting sisters, Hazel, Dot, Persia and Phoebe. Quick to join in were the sleepy-eyed pups, Bewiled and Beepley. A visibly moved Uncle Tunoose then asked for more Senor Fuego in his glass and, once Ma had complied, the old man said, "I feel like doing the Dance of the Jaguar Warrior but this hen an' fur balls'n them pup-mutts have got me down. So I propose a toast instead." Next he held his glass high and when all had done the same, he said:

"Be your own light—shine!"

. . .

Later on, it was just nephew and uncle and the latter was saying, "There's something I've been meaning to ask you. Do you recall when you first started school and your class was told to bring a parent to tell about their job? And because your dad was stationed in Korea I stood in for him and told your teacher and classmates I was a 'pool parlor dude?' Do you recall that?"

"Of course I do. You embarrassed the hell out of me."

"I did that to toughen you up 'cause back then you had a lot of quit in you. But later I felt bad about it'n gave you a Slinky. Then when I saw your Marvin the Martian drawing—"

"You said 'Impressive, nephew, very impressive. You may be a smart aleck kid what's always poppin' off but this shows me you got vision an' imagination, both of which can be worthwhile in this life, even providential.'"

"And you said you could do better, that you wanted to be 'expert' at it."

"Then you told me I had a sense of purpose an' you wanted to promote it, so you gave me some money."

"And now you are expert at your cartoons. Your sense of purpose and vision and imagination make you someone worthwhile and providential."

"That's the nicest thing you've ever said to me, Uncle Tunoose. Do you really mean it?"

"I said it twice didn't I?"

Nephew then said to Uncle, "Much obliged for the hard bark."

. . .

At the Vulcan Gas Company the bands were The Children and New Atlantis. Later that night, Two Moons was composing her first song, "Sugar Shine," when she saw the shadow on her tipi wall. "Hey, haint," she said. "I'm on to you and I gotta a genuine Piegan war tomahawk and I know how to use it."

. . .

AUSTINTACIOUS: A Tale of 1968 Austin

Jack awoke as soon as he heard the thump of the *Austin American* on the front porch. As usual, he looked between him and Jen for Baby Maya. But she was not there and neither was Jen. A wave of alarm swept over him and he sat up in bed to pivot and put his feet on the floor, and this was when he saw Jen peeking out the front porch window. Jen then turned, a finger to her lips to silence Jack as she came over and said in a whisper, "Can you hear it?"

Jack heard a deep mellow voice singing a slow song.

"It's Tunoose," Jen said. "He's singing "Swing Low, Sweet Chariot" to Maya. She loves it."

"I do too."

. . .

A norther blew in Friday morning, November 29 so every gas heater in 200 West 19th Street was going full blast. Maisie was at church. Nubia, Nachita and Monita were outside the tipi bleating to be milked and inside the tipi Two Moons was saying, "There's gonna be cabrito aplenty down at the Town Lake K.O.A. if'n certain ani*mules* don't cut out all that racket." Ryder came to the goats' rescue, though, saying "Hold your horses, Two Moons. I'll milk 'em." Up in the Crow's Nest Abilene was saying, "Oh, look what I found—somebody's got a woody, somebody's got a woody." Whereupon Rosko said, "But do you *seek* it?" Nearby Hannah had Boo Boo—*pwaaak!*—pinned down so as to give the pullet a bath. Down in his bedroom Taj was reading Richard Hittleman's *28-Day Yoga Plan*. Over in Natasha's bedroom the house revolutionary had on her combat boots and a black leotard and was doing a pirouette across the oak plank floor while wondering how she would look in a Joan of Arc haircut. In Jack and Jen's bedroom a flustered Jack was muttering "Oh hell yeah goldurn dogs run free" while trying to spread pages of today's *Austin American* on the floor before Bewiled and Beepley could do their business. On their waterbed a frazzled Jen was trying to soothe a hungry and bawling Baby Maya while wondering why Abilene had not shown up to feed the child. At the same time Bicycle Annie was maneuvering her still somewhat pink

Princess bicycle out of the norther and into the lee of the of the 19th Street house. Once on the wide walkway with "200 W. 19th" stenciled in black paint on its concrete, Annie paused at the bottom of the dozen oak plank steps that went up to the front porch. On the big brass bed she saw Michael A. in his pea coat seated next to a reclined Uncle Tunoose. Holding up a colorful Maya rucksack, Annie said:

"Hey, you two! I got hot chocolate plus bags of 30-cents-a-dozen-day-old donuts! How's that sound?"

"Uncle Tunoose is done for, Annie," a woeful Michael A. said. "He's gone to the Great Beyond, done in by a norther same as Granpa Gage." Then Michael A.'s head sank into his pea coat like a turtle retreating into his shell and he said, "I'll never forget 1968. I've lost Cool Breeze, my dad, my grandfather … and now Uncle Tunoose."

chapter twenty three

Ryder called it "a gathering of the tribe for a rite of passage."

With Nachita, Nubia and Monita grazing in the front yard, Familia Que Tal gathered around their dearly departed loved one. Michael A. helped his Ma into the bentwood rocker then sat beside his uncle on the big brass bed and held Ma's hand. Rosko took a seat on the bed's other side and Bicycle Annie and Taj took the purple butterfly chairs at the end of the bed. Natasha, Jack and a tearful Jen sat on the faded red couch that had been moved out onto the porch for the occasion. Reverent silence held sway until the church ladies arrived to sit behind Aunt Sofi. This was when Two Moons brought out her tom tom, Abilene the washtub bass then Ryder and his sax joined them on the porch steps. Two Moons began to bang her tom tom slowly while Abilene plucked the washtub bass and Ryder's sax blew a blue serenade. Across the street the Gamma Sigs, led by Kilroy and Oily George, brought out their old-timey cannon and fired off a tribute. Mrs. Smalley showed up with Cousin Brucie to whisper soft condolences to Michael A. and his Ma before moving off to one side. Soon a long procession of cars came out of the east on 19th Street to park alongside the curb from Whitis to Wichita Streets. Out of the cars and dressed all in black came the Hyde Park Recreation regulars, friends, business associates and others who had come to pay their respects to Uncle Tunoose. Some held flowers in their hands; many had tears in their eyes. Even the heir-apparent guy from Hyde Park Recreation was there. Respects were paid in Lebanese, Spanish and

English and flowers were left in the lattices at the end of the front porch. Shortly afterwards, the delivery boy from Connelly's Florist started showing up with flowers from all over.

At some point—"to stop my crying"—Jen sang "Swing Low, Sweet Chariot".

To keep from crying, too, all of Que Tal joined in.

It was another big sendoff that would be heard about down in the Big House.

. . .

Jen scooped up a sleeping Maya from beside the also sleeping Jack and went into the entryway and out the front door. She wanted to sit in the low winter sun and begin *The Gay Place*, Billy Brammer's 1962 novel about Austin, but she had not anticipated on Rosko being in one of the purple butterfly chairs. Without looking at them the Elf of Velvet Fortune took his Big Chief tablet in hand and said:

"The sight of you two inspires me." Next, after starting to scribble doodle, he said, "Have I told you how much I like the name Maya Karma Gage? I like it better than Pablo Diego Jose Francisco de Paula la Juan Nepumuceno Maria de los Remedios Cipriano de la Santisima Trinidad Ruiz y Picasso."

Though Jen and Rosko had yet to chat much, Jen took a seat in the bentwood rocker and, after putting Maya on her lap, let the words come. "That's some name," she said. "How'd you get to be just plain ol' 'Rosko'?"

"I earned it. As a child protege, I was pressured to make a name for myself. When I did, I became Rosko."

"Good for you. We should all be who we wanta be."

"A name is but a word." Not looking up from the Big Chief. "Words work wonders in mysterious ways."

Jen smiled and said, "The bird is a word-word-word."

"How nice that you take my meaning," Rosko said and presented his scribble doodle to Jen, who smiled and said:

"Look, Maya, it's a mother and child. It is us."

. . .

On November 30, a Saturday, Michael A., down in the dumps over the passing of his uncle and mentor, happened onto Buck'n Bubba. This semi serendipitous discovery came about when Natasha decided to sell her black Honda 450 motorcycle and so prospective buyer Two Moons took the Honda out for a spin. She followed Michael A. on his burgundy Triumph 650 out Farm to Market Road 2222 and on to Lake Travis's Windy Point then to Hippie Hollow and over Mansfield Dam then back toward town and to The Dry Creek Café. There, after hearing persnickety owner Sara growl into the phone "Of course, I'm open. I answered the blamed phone, didn't I?" then being ordered by Sara to "Bring back your bottles, I'm too old to be waitin' on you," Michael A. and Two Moons went up the rickety wooden stairs to the deck. Here two King Kong-sized brothers introduced themselves as "Buck'n Bubba" from "Earth, Texas, up on the Caprock".

In no time Michael A. was saying, "How providential."

. . .

Jack was down in Songcatcher Studio tuning up his Gibson Melody Maker and Jen and Baby Maya were in their bedroom when Jen heard two voices on the front porch that made her jaw drop.

"Gotta cocuh coluh?" said the first voice.

"Or a Big Red?" said the second.

"Coke and Big Red it is, gents," said Michael A.'s voice "Make yourselves at home while I get 'em."

"Oh my lord, it's your cousins Buck'n Bubba," Jen said to Baby Maya. Then she hurried out of the bedroom with Maya on her shoulder, muttering "Nobody gets to you like your family." In the entryway she encountered a grinning Michael A. who said to her:

"Ya got kinfolk come callin' from Earth, up on the Caprock."

"What was that about the Caprock?" said Jack now coming up the stairs.

Michael A. said, "Sister Woman's got company what hail from there. And guess what? These ol' boys was reconnaissance pilots in Nam."

"Fascinatin'," Jack said. "Mighty fascinatin'."

After sticking her tongue out at Michael A., Jen and Maya went through the screen door onto the front porch where, not giving it much, Jen said, "Terdell. Doolittle. What a surprise. How nice of y'all to pay a visit."

"Well, hey, lookee here, Bubba, it's Cousin Jennifer!" said Buck, getting up from a purple butterfly chair.

"Talk about your small world," Bubba said, getting up from the other purple butterfly chair. "Good lord, is that young'un yours, Cousin Jennifer?"

"She is. Wanta make somethin' of it?"

"Shucks no," said Buck. "But I don't believe anybody back in Earth knew you was even knocked up."

"Boy howdy, tongues are sure gonna wag now," Bubba said.

"How're your folks?" Jen said. "They in fine fettle?"

"Hardly," Buck said. "Poppa's got the misery on accounta he got drunk an' done run the pickup into the bar ditch."

"So Momma's got Poppa," said Bubba.

"About which Momma ain't happy," Buck said.

"An' when Momma ain't happy, ain't nobody happy," Bubba said.

Michael A. and Jack now came out onto the porch with a "cocuh coluh" for Buck and a Big Red for Bubba, Michael A. saying, "Might you boys need a place to crash?" Winking at Jen as he said, "Seein' as how y'all're family an' it's family first in this old house."

"Why, thank ya kindly," Buck said.

"I can flop right here on the porch," said Bubba.

"Is that big brass bed taken?" said Buck.

"Have at it," said Michael A. "Out with the old, in with the new."

"Just where up on the Caprock is Earth?" Jack said.

"East of Muleshoe'n south of Hereford," said Buck.

"Our Dairy Queen's got the bestest durn root beer float in alla Texas," said Bubba.

A wildly grinning Michael A. said, "And just what brings ya'll ta Austin?"

"Like we said—we need money," Buck said.

Jack said, "For a farm up on the Caprock?"

Bubba said, "Nope, no honey-pond-with-a-flapjack-tree-in-it notions for us."

"We aim to buy two crop dustin' planes," Buck said.

"Mighty fine place ya got here," Bubba said. "Is y'all rich hippies?"

"Oh my lord,," Jen said, rolling her eyes, "here we go."

. . .

They were in the Night Hawk Restaurant at 23rd and Guadelupe, Buck saying, "Much obliged" as he bolted down the last of his steak and omelet.

"That goes double for me, Michael A.," Bubba said. "I flat out don't think I could stomach that 'earth food' Cousin Jennifer was fixin' ta feed us."

"That gal eats like a bird, always has," Buck said. "She's pure D namby pamby when it comes to vittles."

"Real men need meat," said Bubba.

"Leastwise some*thin*' with stayin' power," said Buck.

"Not that rabbit food whut goes through ya like grits through a goose," said Bubba.

Michael A. took a sip of his Superior Dairies Homogenized Milk and said, "Now tell me more about this red-haired *sinsemilla* connection you mentioned."

"Well-sir," Buck said, "in Nam we was buddies with a guy what's got people in Old Mexico who'll front mota."

"An another of his kinfolks is an *el general* whut commands an air base in Oaxaca," Bubba said. "An' for a fee we can load up'n fly outta there."

Bubba said, "But we got nobody to off the mota."

"Sock it to me," Michael A. said. "You got a plane?"

"There's planes in Bastrop we can, uh, borrow," Buck said.

"Just go at the right time an' fly away," Bubba said with a wink.

Michael A. said, "Where would you land the mota?"

"Right here in town," said Buck.

"At that new freeway they're buildin'," Bubba said.

"Mopac Expressway?" Michael A. said. Next, after a brief pause, he said, "I like it. I also got a commercial mind *annnd* I'm feeling raunchy'n persnickety with a wild hair to boot. Sooo, because 'no risks, no riches' is the name of the game"—pausing to raise his half pint carton of Superior Dairies Homogenized Milk and catch his breath—"I say here's to success, to crime." Then, after Buck and Bubba had grinned and nodded, he said:

"Did Jen eat her boogers when she was a kid?"

chapter twenty four

Bicycle Annie handed Michael A. two Texas driver's licenses—one for Maynard G. Krebbs, one for I.B. Gilligan—and said, "Mopac Expressway was named after the Missouri Pacific railroad that runs through there. It was planned in 1961 when Austin was 160,000 folks and construction on its 45th street interchange begins in February. Your old house on Elba Place is up on concrete blocks and must be moved because of imminent domain."

Michael A. said, "Thanx, Annie. You're always up on current events. Now what's My Lai and the *USS Liberty*?"

"Word on the street is our guys massacred hundreds of old men, women and children in My Lai village. A Lieutenant Calley and Captain Medina are being blamed."

A stunned Miguel Antonio Medina did not hear what Annie said about the *USS Liberty*.

. . .

"Don't worry about what you can't control" his dad used to tell him. So Michael A. went back to work by hitting up the three lock box for what he figured would be sufficient funds. After stuffing the moolah in his Levis, he rode his Triumph 650 to Highland Park Drug. There he used the pay phone to call the number on the real estate sign in front of his former home and inquire about 1019 Elba Place. The real estate agent gave his spiel and an asking price. Michael A. countered that he knew that this was a time sensitive transaction, that 1019 Elba Place had to be moved soon. Next he offered half the asking price—"cash money in your hand today"—and half an hour later Maynard G. Krebbs was a new homeowner.

. . .

Michael A. was telling Jack on the front porch of the 19th Street house, "I lived in 1019 Elba Place. Remember? When my dad was at Camp Mabry."

"Sure, I remember," Jack said. "It had a sand box where me'n the girl next door played doctor."

"Really? How come I wasn't in on that?"

"You had the chicken pox."

"Bummer."

"So you're gonna offload 1350 kilos of red-haired sinsemilla right into your old home?"

"Yep. It's all set down in Oaxaca. Buck'n Bubba'll land the loads one after the other in their borrowed Cessnas in the middle of the night on a weekday. They plan to fly over the Gulf of Mexico an' come into the U.S. over Houston so as to get lost in its air traffic. We offload an' the planes are back in Bastrop less than twenty four hours later."

"You know those two ol' boys is rough as corn cobs, doncha?"

"Yep. Genuine yahoos. But those two sod-bustin' clodhoppers is also family."

"Who gets the mota?"

"Cacciatore. He says he'll cash out both loads. Says he'll use a Yellow Freight truck'n hide the mota behind a wall of boxed up color TVs he's gonna buy from Oscar Snowden down on Congress Avenue."

Jack said, "Color TVs, huh? I ain't yet seen what one a them can do."

"They do fine'n dandy. Cacciatore figures to make a killing on em 'cause TV's just now coming to Aspen."

"You know what, Cuz?"

"What?"

"I think I'd like one of them color TVs. It's gettin' right crowded around the Stromberg Carlson."

"Tell me about it."

AUSTINTACIOUS: A Tale of 1968 Austin

. . .

They were at Dead Meat Barbeque off Comal Street in East Austin where, for $1.50, Cool Breeze's granmomma and momma had served up barbequed spare ribs, sauce, tater salad, red beans and pickles and onions with a pitcher of iced tea. Dessert was a double helping of "Nanner Puddin."

"We'll do 'er next norther," said Buck, mouth full of everything on his plate.

"That way we can both land'n take off into the wind," said Bubba, his mouth dripping sauce.

"The planes won't make much racket when landing," said Buck.

"But them engines'll sure be a-whinin'n grindin' on take-off," Bubba said.

Next they went to Academy Surplus on Interstate 35 across from Hancock Plaza. There they bought eight Coleman lanterns to serve as landing lights.

"We'll keep the lanterns're in their boxes," said Buck.

"That's so the lights're only seen from above," said Bubba.

"The boxes won't catch fire?" said Michael A.

Buck looked at Bubba and said, "Didn't think of that, didcha, idgit?"

"Well, you didn't neither, dummo."

"We'll put tin foil in the boxes' insides," said Michael A.

. . .

The next norther was forecast for Sunday through Tuesday, so the smuggle was planned for after midnight Monday. Buck'n Bubba and Michael A. had just finished walking up and down their makeshift air strip to remove obstacles that could cause damage to a plane. Now they were in the pink Caddy going home and Buck was saying:

"When you hear two clicks on the radio, we're almost here. *Click* pause *click* an' it's show time."

Bubba said, "You an' your buddy bring out his Yellow Freight truck, the three of you offload then do 'er again with me later."

After midnight that Monday, Michael A. placed the Coleman lanterns in their tin-foil-lined boxes along the eastern edge of the strip. Then he waited in Elba Place beside the air to ground radio. Over and over he sang:

"Blowww, you old blue norther."

. . .

While waiting for the *click*-pause-*click* Cacciatore and Michael A. sat on the latter's first ever bed while the former jabbered, first, about scoring a missile silo then about running for sheriff of Pitkin County.

"If I'm sheriff we can land loads on the mesa I got near Crotchkiss then stash the loads in the missile silo. What a hidey-hole—can't see it topside and its got an elevator that goes 200 feet down into the earth."

Despite the norther, Cacciatore wore a fuchia Hawaiian shirt, scarlet Bermuda shorts, water buffalo sandals, a white fedora hat and mirror shades. Michael A. was more nondescript. He had on a sweatshirt, jeans, his white Converse tennies and his Navy pea coat.

The lapel of the pea coat did sport a button saying "Reality is a crutch," though.

chapter twenty five

"Look away. I am hideous."

"No, you're not, Taj," Two Moons said. "We all got scars, inside and out. Wanta see where Whooping Coyote whacked me in the head with a golf club?"

"No, but why did he do that?"

"It was my fault. I got in the way of his back swing." Then she said, "Now suck it."

After doing as told, Taj said, "Most pleasant."

"You like it fine, huh?"

"Yes, and in spite of Michael A.'s perverse manner of instruction."

"Same here. He has a way of sexing everything up. But after a few trips to Caruso's I got the hang of it an' now I like crawdads just fine."

"I find it not unlike consuming escargot or oysters."

"I haven't done either one of those," said Two Moons.

"Then we must soon enjoy those pleasures as well."

"Oh my goodness. Mud bugs now, snails an' oysters next. The tribe'll wonder if Austin's got me speaking with a forked tongue."

"There is nothing forked about an educated palate, is there?"

"Nope. Not for an open mind."

. . .

Taj was in his room doing one-armed pushups when Michael A. appeared in the doorway and said:

"Hey! Mr. Pleasant Presence! First I lose Natasha to you an' now you're with Two Moons. How come you're stealing my ladies?"

"I do not steal them," Taj said, grunting through his efforts. "I win them."

"Opinions vary, Everyman. I say it ain't cool."

"If you leave it you lose it. House Rule Number Two."

"I didn't leave nobody! They left *me!*"

"It matters not," Taj said after another grunt, "since we cooled the rules."

. . .

Baby Maya's wet nurses sat in the purple butterfly chairs on the front porch. They were talking shop.

"She's a biter," Two Moons said.

Abilene said, "She's got plenty of pucker power too. She could suck the chrome off a John Deere tractor hitch."

"And, ohhh," Two Moons said, wincing, "the pain from those itty bitty fingernails digging into your chest."

"Or her kick to the nose with that wicked right foot."

"Or the ear. Yep, that papoose has got quite a reach."

Abilene said, "I can only use my left one 'cause my right one's shopworn."

"That little gal's been ridin' me hard too."

"Michael A. calls us 'Maya's Dynamic Duos.'"

"Yeah, an' I call *him* 'Victor Voyeur'," said Two Moons. "He claims he has to watch Maya feed on account of he's her Quality Control Officer."

"He's a pain."

"Him and Maya both."

"Not to worry, ladies," said Jen, walking out onto the front porch with a baby bottle in her hand. "I hereby declare Maya Karma Gage officially weaned and Victor Voyeur relieved of Quality Control."

"Victor Voyeur ain't gonna like that," said Two Moons, grinning.

"Maya Karma Gage ain't gonna like it none neither," said Abilene.

"'Tough titty' said the kitty."

It was not their first quart of Old Milwaukee when Michael A. said, "It's beer thirty" and took a proffered church key from Jack to open another quart. After taking a big slug he handed the quart to Buck.

"So how was it for you, Michael A.?" Buck said after taking a swig and handing the quart to Bubba.

"How was what?"

"Your hitch with Uncle Sam," said Bubba, passing the quart to Jack.

"Oh, that. Well, in the army I didn't have to do any thinking. But out here in the Real World my life revolves around a thousand petty hassles."

"And what about this here boy?" Buck said, nodding at Taj now joining them on the front porch. "Me'n Bubba been wonderin' if he was in Nam."

"'Cause he sure looks like he was," said Bubba, looking at where Taj's arm had been.

"He's for sure been to hell and back," Michael A. said.

"But it was a motorcycle wreck that took his arm," said Jack.

Then everyone looked at Taj who said, "Did you know that in New Hampshire from 1832 to 1835 there was a 280-square-mile independent nation?"

"I know one thing," Bubba said to Taj. "You're full of useless information."

Buck said, "I bet he aims to be one of them Piled Higher'n Deeper types."

"I thought it was 'Piled Higher'n Dryer'," Bubba said.

Taj said, "Frankly, fellows, I am twixt hither and yon about being a PhD candidate."

"Do tell," Buck said. Then, looking at the jeans of his hosts, he said, "How come y'all Austintacious types wear them namby pamby Levis?"

"Yeah," Bubba said. "Our Wrangler jeans is cheaper."

"An' they're also high Panhandle fashion," said Buck.

Jack said, "Wranglers have a serious shortcoming."

Buck said, "An' that shortcoming'd be what?"

"They're like a small town hotel," Michael A. said.

"How's that?" said Bubba.
"They got no ball room."

. . .

Apres sex, the lovers continued to lie still, as still and as bare as when they had breathed their first breath in this all too brief tantalization called Life. They lay side by side as if they were on, not his small mattress, but a white sand beach bordering an azure sea lapping and licking at that beach as much as he had recently lapped and licked at the lanky beauty with languid eyes who lay beside him. These lovers lay still beneath a morning sun reflecting off the dreamcatcher in the north window. She lay on her stomach, her legs extended fully, her arms folded beneath her chin for a head rest. He lay beside her on his right side, his body also fully extended. His right arm was bent, his head supported by the palm of his right hand. Though her head was turned toward him, her eyes were held shut by the weight of tepid bliss from him stroking her backside with a long caresses in a drawn out rhythm. He caressed her by dragging his hair down her back, his stroke from her shoulders to her waist as close to being a sensuous, sumptuous breeze as touch can get. For him nothing seemed finer in the human form than the backside of a woman. Nor was anything more pleasing to the eye and libido, a primal vision of sacred beauty, a path to heaven as pleasing as the feather touch the long delicate strokes his hair gave her, a warmth there born of desire and fire. The Language of Touch was indeed the Consummate Pleasure of Sensuality. Abilene broke the mood, however, when she said from her prone position behind them:

"Some threesome. No fair, Two Moons—you're hoggin' the huggin'. An' turn this way, willya, Taj, so you can give *me* some of that good lovin'."

. . .

The pale moonlight was painting pictures in the sky above the portions of the inner city where urban darkness dwelled among the shadows of walls and extended eaves of old rooftops. When the norther had blown in and What Goes Bump In The Night had felt its chill, he built another fire. Once it was lit, The Voice said:

"Darkness is a heart turned upside down and loneliness is its shadow, so hear me, feel me, touch me, you who flash me up and down with your light."

What Goes Bump In The Night's reply was to sneer and say, "You, the goats, dogs, squirrels and that darned cat and chicken are gonna be the end of me."

. . .

The next morning Ryder was milking Nubia when Natasha walked over to him and said, "I was raised on goat's milk."

"Good stuff, goat's milk" was all Ryder said, being careful with this woman who had been unusually cool toward him since the Wreck of the Fitty Six. Now, however, she was getting up close and personal with him, even seemed to smell him before saying:

"That's a musty odor ya got, Ryder. Do I know you, Ryder? Or maybe I should say 'Did you knowww *me*?'"

"It's just patchouli oil, ma'am. I'll quit wearin' it if ya don't care for it."

chapter twenty six

It was Sunday, December 1. Baby Maya was at church with Ma and the church ladies and Jack and Jen were alone on their waterbed reading the Sunday paper. Jen was reading Dear Abby and Jack was enjoying the funny papers. He was chuckling at Linus in Peanuts when Jen said:

"Jaaack, do you love me?"

"Yes, ma'am. First an' foremost an' forever."

"Do you remember how Boo Boo brought out my maternal instincts?" Then she batted her sapphire eyes, smiled her perfect smile and said, "For me that was like xutan for pregnancy … if you get my meaning."

It took a while, but finally Jack said, "Really?"

"Yep. Are you in for the long haul, Cowboy?"

"I'm in an' you're *onnn*, Cowgirl. On top that is."

"And they say you can't even lead a jackass to water."

"'Happy is the man, and happy he alone,
He who can call today his own,
He who, secure within, can say
Tomorrow do thy worst, for I have lived today,
Be for or foul, rain or shine,
The joys I have possessed, in spite of fate, are mine,
Not Heaven itself upon the past has power,
But what has been has been and I have had my hour'"

"Cool," Jen said. "Now you gimme *myyy* hour, Ben Jack Gage."

On the floor in front of the faded red couch the headline for December 2 was that the UN General assembly had voted to condemn South Africa for its apartheid policy. But up on the couch Michael A. was holding either Jack or Jen's Early Childhood Education text book and saying to the infant on his lap:

"Okay, Maya, you're now three months old an' if you're healthy'n all like that, according to this text book, you're sposed to mimic facial expressions during playtime." Michael A. then made a goofy face a la Soupy Sales and right away Baby Maya's face registered a reaction. "Goood girl. Next you're sposed to babble an' mimic my sounds." Michael A. then said, "Goo goo kachoo" and Baby Maya did, too, sort of. "Goood girl." Michael A. now looked again at the text book and said, "No need to support your head anymore. 'On stomach can lift head and chest'—check. 'A little pushup for rolling over'—check. 'Open and clap hands'—check. 'Hands to mouth'—double check. 'Push down with legs'—ditto." Michael A. then closed the text book and said, "So far, so good, kiddo, and as a reward you'n me're gonna watch "Dark Shadows." Then he whispered:

"But don't tell Jen."

. . .

It was 3 A.M., Wednesday, December 4, a full moon. It was break time in Songcatcher Studio and, as usual, there was a line of housemates waiting to use the downstairs bathroom.

"What I have here is a failure to concentrate," Michael A. said. He was third in line and behind Buck'n Bubba. "In this crowded house not only do I stand in line to go to the can but I sleep on a couch in the living room an' thus I am the first one up'n the last one to bed."

"And what do you deduce from that?" said Two Moons who was behind him in line.

"I deduce that familiarity is breeding contempt."

Taj now came out of the bathroom, let Buck go in past him, and said, "'Familiarity breeds contempt' is from Aesop's fable The Fox and the Lion."

Michael A. ignored this to look at the line behind him and say, "I suggest we take a census. Let's see, our permanent residents are me the sole surviving son an' Taj the foreign student. Then there's Jack an' Jen, our lovers-what-got-their own-bathroom. There's Natasha, our revolutionary who also has her own bathroom. For moochers we got the Kong Brothers, Buck'n Bubba, who're so huge they oughta count as two people each. And, oh yeah, we also got Mona the Haint. Then we got Ryder an' Bicycle Annie always hangin' around bein' helpful. Wet Willie's here a lot but he's always welcome. Finally we got a runaway named Abilene floppin' here, there an' everywhere plus a Piegan princess what lives out back in a tipi-what's-got-a-privy."

"And which happens to be a long walk from Songcatcher Studio," said Two Moons.

"Anyway," Michael A. said, "I figure our house has thirteen denizens."

"*Presente*," said Rosko as he and Michael A.'s Ma got in line.

"Oops. Make that fifteen denizens'n one spirit."

"I hope you didn't forget Tiny dancer and Rain Shadow," Ma said. "Also The Dry Spot In A Wet Place and The Voice By The Fire."

"That makes—oh, shoot, I've lost count," Michael A. said. Which was when Buck came out of the bathroom and right away everybody in line reached up to hold his or her nose.

"Use the kitchen matches!" said Michael A.

"Everything come out alright, bro?" said Bubba.

"Good as it gets, Bub."

"Clean break, huh?"

"Yep. No back door trots, no skid marks, no butt rust."

"Didn't plug up the plumbin' this time?"

"I did. But warn't no plumber's helper in sight."

"And oh-my-lord what a revoltin' development this is," said Michael A.

. . .

Taj's Motorola was playing Radio Reefer playing Tiny Tim's "Tip-Toe Thru The Tulips With Me" for Michael A. in his hamaca up in the

Crow's Nest. He was watching Hannah trying to engage a squirrel atop the first chimney, but the squirrel was not into it. And when Hannah ran at the squirrel, it darted down the chimney with Hannah hot on its trail.

"Whoa!" Michael A. said then heard Taj yell from down in his room:

"Who goes there?"

So down the spiral staircase Michael A. went, past the dreamcatcher in the window and into Taj's room.

"I heard noises in the attic," Taj said.

"Hannah's chased a squirrel down the chimney," Michael A. said and next they heard Natasha say:

"Ouu spooky."

So Taj and Michael A. rushed through the bathroom that connected to Natasha's bedroom and into the entryway. Here they saw Natasha in the living room. She pointed at the floor-to-ceiling bookcase and said:

"I heard noises in there."

They then heard Ryder downstairs saying, "Hey, Hannah, what're you doing in there?" Next Michael A., Taj and Natasha were with Ryder and Hannah in Songcatcher Studio and Ryder was saying:

"Hannah was in the Teac's closet."

"Was the squirrel with her?" said Michael A.

"I didn't see any squirrel," Ryder said. Now looking into the closet, he said, "But I can see that Hannah got through the wall via a panel in the closet's brick wall. The panel swings open into an air shaft. Also, some of the shaft's bricks are offset to make a spiral ascent. I can see daylight above but no sky."

Natasha said, "I guess the closet was once a fireplace."

"The one Mona met her death in?" said Michael A.

. . .

They were in her tipi cuddled up beneath a buffalo robe when he nudged her and said, "Good morning, Sunshine."

"*Ya basta* with the rumpy pumpy, Michael A.," Two Moons said. She waited until he had backed off her before saying, "Is 'Sunshine' what you call that thing?"

"I don't call it anything. I was only greeting the day."

"My psychology professor says men tend to name the body part that makes most of their decisions."

"Jen had that professor and she's a lesbian terrorist." Next he leaned back to clasp his hands behind his head and say, "Ya know, tipi living ain't bad when ya got electricity an' a privy." Giving her a wink, he said, "Sure beats a faded red couch."

"So get your own tipi and we'll share the electricity and privy."

"Awww"—sounding hurt—"don't you love me, Two Moons?"

"To quote you: 'What's love got to do with it? I make you feel good, you do the same for me.'" Then she got out of bed saying, "I got class."

"Of course you do. You're a classy gal."

"Psy*chol*ogy class, you hipster-doofus-jive-ass-creepy-womanizer-twisted satyr."

Michael A. was pretty sure that last part was pure D Jen.

. . .

On the morning of December 7, a Saturday, Two Moons, Ryder and Mrs. Smalley were by the tipi milking the goats when Bicycle Annie rode into the driveway on her still somewhat new Princess bicycle. "Today is Pearl Harbor Day," Annie said. "Twenty-seven years ago the Japanese attacked us with 353 aircraft from six aircraft carriers. The Japanese lost but 64 men while we lost—"

"2403 Americans," Mrs. Smalley said. "I know because one of them was my husband."

chapter twenty seven

It was also on Pearl Harbor Day that Michael A. ran out of pot, mota, grass, weed, ganja, Mary Jane, boo, Choice Quality Stuff, God bud. It happened while Abilene was snoring on the faded red couch, while Radio Reefer's Deejay Everyman was spinning Roy Orbison's "Only the Lonely" on the Monkey Ward's stereo in the living room, while Natasha was in her room cursing blue blazes to no one but herself, while Jack and Jen were in their bedroom talking baby talk to Baby Maya and while Buck'n Bubba, Two Moons, Ryder and Bicycle Annie were gabbing and cackling on the front porch as Nachita, Nubia and Monita were on the porch steps bleating to be milked. It was a fed-up, melted down Michael A. at the church-door-turned-dining-room table who told Thelma and Barney Lou and family:

"I can't even hear myself think."

. . .

That Saturday night Shiva's Head Band and Bubble Puppy were at the Vulcan Gas Company. Between bands Michael A. and Rosko stepped outside, bummed about being unable to partake of their usual sacrament.

"Mota gets you through times of no lana better than lana gets you through times of no mota," Rosko said.

"Amen to that," Michael A. said. "I'm in a humongous funk, Rosko. I'm shortin' out, I'm downspinnin' into a frenzy—I can't get no relief.

Back at the house My Space in Time is the eye of the storm. Radio Reefer's goin' full blast four feet away so I can't even practice The Fine Art of Hanging Out or be one of nature's layabouts. I can't work out the bass line to "Paint It Black," can't work on my screenplay *I Am Yellow(Jello)*. It's too cold for me in the Crow's Nest, the pink Caddy an' the VW bus. The bathroom I have to share reeks like a feed lot an' no amount of kitchen matches'll kill the stink. 19th an' University's a crash pad. I gotta get out of that place if it's the last thing I ever do."

Rosko said, "What is time, Michael A.?"

"A traveler on the Road," he said, catching on right away. "Good one, Rosko, time being relative to experience. The bus station's right across the street an' I couldn't be feelin' more freewheelin'. Leave us bus to San Antonio an' take the train. East or west don't make me no never mind as I got loose ends to tie up both ways."

"I suggest we go west, young man, and see friends in Big Sur, Santa Cruz and San Francisco. But going by bus and train is the European way. Why not go native?"

"I'm hip," Michael A. said. "We'll drive."

. . .

Later that night in the driveway of the 19th Street house could be heard a chant, a primal mantra that went:

"*Road Trip! Road Trip! Road Trip!*"

Rosko was by the 1968 Maya blue T-Bird wearing a Yucatecan straw hat, white linen slacks, chanclas and a pea coat over a Maya blue cowboy shirt with pearl-topped buttons. As he danced a fandango with one arm swinging free, he said to Michael A., "We drive by night and play by day, yes?"

"Okay by me," said Michael A. He had on mirror shades, Levis, chanclas and wore his officer's pea coat over a T-shirt that said **SE-CEDE**. In the T-Bird's trunk and next to Jen's two empty olive green Samsonite suitcases were his handwoven, beaded elkskin medicine bag, golf clubs from Big John's House of Crap and Rosko's Maya rucksack. In the T-Bird's back seat Jen, Abilene and Two Moons were filling a cooler with Oedibles eats, half pint cartons of Superior Dairies

Homogenized Milk and a Mason jar of Tejas Indian Tea made from Treaty Oak acorns and Yucatecan honey. Meanwhile, Jack was placing a bottle of Senor Fuego tequila beneath the driver's bucket seat as Taj put the Purple Crab kite on the console and a leather pouch full of Texas Medicine in the glove box. When Natasha gave the thumbs-up that she had replaced the T-Bird's legal license plates with the ones stolen from Oily George, Bicycle Annie nodded then turned to Michael A. and said:

"You got the title and registration?"

"Yep. Maynard G. Krebbs keeps 'em in the console."

"You're taking the back roads?"

"Yep. All the way to this bewildering republic's only one of the Seven Wonders of the World."

. . .

It was dawn in Lawn, Texas, and Rosko was having tea while studying a road map. After taking a sip, he said:

"At Tuscola we take Highway 613 to Buffalo Gap then to Noodle. Unusual names, but every place is home to someone."

"We need to talk, Rosko."

"But not about cabbages and kings, eh, Michael A.? And let us please keep in mind that the key to talk is listening, that it is pointless to look for the answer so much as the real question and that good ideas never die of old age."

"Check. Now fess up about why you put that pouch of 'diamonds from the African mines' in my medicine bag."

"Ah, the baudy baubles. My gift to the transcendent beings of Que Tal. Not sought but found. I feel sure you shall use them wisely."

"But what's Que Tal to you?"

"You are the truth and you have helped set us free."

"'Us?'"

"Nacho, Tunoose and me. Experiencing Que Tal has been a rebirth for us. You have restored our youth, maybe even our former glory. You inspire."

"You sound like a groupie."

"*Yesss*, that's what we are. We are your groupies. Que Tal's idealism and altruism always aim for a Greater Good. Namely, saving the planet from The Virus That Is Us."

"One planet! One world."

"One world! One planet. Fortune smiles upon you, so smile back. Shine a light."

"How?"

"By being you. Nacho likened Que Tal to a reincarnation of la maya's Hero Twins, the young jaguar warriors who helped bring the past into the present so as to light the way forward. If the lessons of the past are to be learned then the future—you, Que Tal—must quest for answers." Rosko's elfish smile now shined as he chanted:

By the River of Time,
On the Isle of Swallows,
Did you not find the way?
Did you not teach the bold?
Shall you not BE again?
Shall you not LEAD again?
Every ending is a beginning
On the Isle of Swallows,
By the River of Time

"Heavy," Michael A. said.

"Very," Rosko said and after taking another sip of his acorn tea said, "Enjoy the ride."

. . .

The T-Bird made its way up to Noodle then over to Roby and Highway 180. From there it was straight across the rest of Texas: Snyder, Gail, Lamesa, Seminole into Hobbs, New Mexico. By now Rosko had learned from the T-Bird's Owner's Manual that their bucket seats would fully recline, so they parked beneath a cottonwood tree in Harry McAdams State park and grabbed some shuteye. Next they did the forty-two miles to Loco Hills and had burritos and beer at a roadside cantina on Highway 82. They then cruised through Artesia, Hope, Elk, Mayhill up to 8700 feet at Cloudcroft and down the steep grade through Mountain Park and High Rolls. After turning onto Highway 54 it was full tilt boogie north through Tularosa to near Three Rivers. Here Rosko went ape over a sign that said "Petroglyphs" and pointed east down a dirt road. Not long afterwards, at Three Rivers National Petroglyph Site, the bucket seats were again fully reclined and more shuteye was grabbed.

An hour after nibbling on some of Oedibles' couscous a la Taj, Rosko was running wild amongst the petroglyph-covered rocks. The old one had gone back in time, hundreds of petroglyphs having been etched into the rocks of this escarpment that provided a commanding view of the surrounding plain. This primitive art depicted Nature's beings—humans, birds, snakes, deer and other herd animals—as a celebration of the site itself. Here ancient tribes had been able to chart their prey's route from far enough away to plot where they could intersect their prey for the hunt or battle. Whoever controlled the rocks controlled this part of the world.

"Always take the high ground," Rosko said.

And when Rosko found a rock etched with the image of a duck above an arrow pointing southwest, he rejoiced by dancing a flamenco and shouting, *"What it is is what it was! What it was is what it is!"* For the arrow pointed at a pond in the distance and on this pond he and Michael A. had seen ducks gathering. Rosko was so inspired that he used the rest of the afternoon to scribble doodle in his Big Chief tablet. And when Michael A. got a look at Rosko's efforts, he saw optical illusions: three Don Quixotes that could also be read "Nacho," "Tunoose" and "Rosko."

. . .

An hour before sunset they returned to Highway 54 and continued north through Oscura to Carrizozo then went west on Highway 380 as the sun set beyond the volcanic badlands called Valley of

Fires. After dusk they continued west through Bingham beyond which—south—was the chalk-like glow of White Sands Missile Range where the first atomic bomb had been detonated on July 16, 1945.

"A show like that cost a bundle," Michael A. said.

Rosko, however, refused to look.

In Socorro they turned onto Highway 60 and gained altitude as they drove through Magdalena, Datil, past Madre Mountain's 9,560-foot-high peak to Pie Town. Here they stopped and over rhubarb pie became embroiled in a real life rhubarb between the cook and a Navajo waitress. It ended when the latter cast aside her apron then came over to whisper in Rosko's ear.

"She wants a ride to The Rez," said the Elf of Velvet Fortune.

Michael A. shrugged and said, "The more the merrier."

In Quemado, just past Omega, Barba Una, as she called herself, met up with her sister Barba Dos, another waitress fed up with her employment situation. Soon both sisters were headed home in the T-Bird and Michael A. was saying to them:

"Barba Una an' Barba Dos, huh?"

"Yep," Barba Una said, "and we call the youngest in our family Barba Diez."

"Ten kids? Not much Zero Population Growth on The Rez, is there?"

"Nope, no newfangled notions on The Rez," said Barba Dos.

"But it is a sovereign nation," said Barba Una.

Michael A. thought a moment and said, "Does this sovereign nation of yours have a straight road?"

"Straight as an arrow and flat as a tortilla," said Barba Dos.

"Good to know," said Michael A., getting an idea.

"I really like your T-Bird," Barba Una said.

"So do I," Barba Dos said.

"Thanks, but what I'd *really* like for a set of wheels is a fastback Mustang like Steve McQueen had in *Bullit*."

. . .

Having recently been waitresses, Las Barba chicas were loaded with quarters and other change so it was easy to for Michael A. to call Austin from the pay phone at The Petrified Forest gift shop, get Sara of the Dry Creek Cafe on the line and tell her:

"Put Buck'n Bubba on the line'n I guaran-damn-tee-ya they'll make it worth your while."

. . .

It was a purple majesty's dawn with a skyborn Purple Crab kite to boot. Though the temperature was thirty-six degrees, Cacciatore's attire was still a fuchia Hawaiian shirt, scarlet Bermuda shorts, water buffalo sandals, a white fedora hat and mirror shades. The Beatles' "Hello Goodbye" was playing on his Volkswagen bus's radio and from its antenna the Purple Crab kite flew over the South Rim of the Grand Canyon, the USA's only one of the Seven Wonders of the World. Inside the VW bus were Jen's Samsonite suitcases atop 300 kilos of red-haired sinsemilla. Outside the bus stood Michael A. in his pea coat looking worried as he said:

"If Uncle Tunoose has said it once, he's said it a jillion times— 'No mota with the moolah' *ever!*"

"Relax, soon you'll be on the train thinking about that missile silo," Cacciatore said. Then he yelled "*Fore!,*" swung his golf club and—*thwaaack!*—the small white ball went zooming far out into the canyon's majestic abyss.

It had been one sweet smuggle: Bubba called el general who said 300 kilos was ready and waiting, so Buck "borrowed" a plane then flew under the radar across the border to get lost in the Tucson-Phoenix air traffic before landing on a Petrified Forest straightaway lit by the headlights of the T-Bird and the VW bus. Once the cargo was unloaded, the Barba sisters got the T-Bird from Michael A. and a bale of sinsemilla from Cacciatore.

Michael A. was now saying to Cacciatore, "You said that Signe's dumping me because she thinks I'm *what?*"

"Ostentatious," Caccciatore said as he stoked up a Thai Stick in his cigarette holder.

"But she lives in Aspen. It doesn't get any more ostentatious than that."

Cacciatore exhaled a stream of Thai smoke and said, "Your godawful ugly toes were also mentioned."

This was when they heard Rosko say, "*Oye!* Look what I find" which caused Michael A. to look that way and say:

"Oops. Not at all providential, Rosko."

"*Au contraire, mon frère,*" Cacciatore said. "That's the Grand Canyon rattlesnake Rosko has found and it is a stellar example of Darwin's Theory of Evolution because its pink color allows it to survive predatory birds by blending in with the canyon's equally pink rocks." Cacciatore then looked over at Michael A. and said, "You should appeal more to a woman's instincts. It wears 'em down."

"Nahhh, that just ain't me. I'm gracious to a fault."

chapter twenty eight

The second week of December was final exams. On December 10 Jen went against Natasha's wishes and told Jack, "Natasha got raped in the alley the night of the Wreck of the Fitty Six. She's pregnant but doesn't want to go the back alley abortion route."

"Ouu, no. Lawsy mercy, nooo."

"So she's suckered Oily George into thinking the kid's his an' tonight she's getting an abortion at a society doctor's house on Balcones Drive. I'm going with her."

"I'll go too."

"No, you won't."

"Why not? She's my friend too."

"Because you have to look after our daughter."

"Oh. Right."

. . .

On the morning of December 11, Taj had just read in the *Austin American* that the unemployment rate was 3.3 percent—the lowest in fifteen years—when he opened the upstairs bathroom door in his room to find Natasha slumped on the floor and written in blood on the bathroom wall was:

Asses to asses
Lust to lust
Ashes to ashes
Dust to dust

. . .

In the hospital waiting room, Jen came in and said to Taj, Jack, Abilene, Two Moons, Bicycle Annie and Ryder, "Natasha's hemorrhaging badly so we gotta give blood."

Soon after Taj learned that he was a Universal Donor.

Four hours later Jen returned to the waiting room and told everybody, "She's gonna make it."

. . .

For December 12 at the Vulcan Gas Company were New Atlantis and a group from Dallas that included Jimmie Vaughn, Denny Freeman and Paul Ray. Half way through their set, the kid next to Jack said to him:

"The lead guitar player's my big brother Jimmie."

Jack said, "Well, he sure shows a fine feeling in his fingers."

. . .

On Route 66 in downtown Flagstaff, Arizona, Michael A. was in line to buy their train tickets to California when Rosko came out of a jewelry store. As he handed Michael A. the money for the tickets, he said, "See what I find" and pointed across the street to the Motel Du Beau on 19 West Phoenix Street. At first, Michael A. thought that Rosko was pointing at the Du Beau's fifty-foot high sign, but then he saw an identical-in-every-way-to Steve McQueen' fastback Mustang parked by the Du Beau office. Seeing it had a For Sale sign on it, Michael A. picked up Jen's Samsonites and headed that way saying:

"Man oh man, talk about life imitating art."

. . .

High on new-car joy, Michael A. drove his newly acquired Mustang all night and half the next day. In Sequoia National Park they slept beside a giant Sequoia. In Yosemite National Park they peeked out from behind Bridalveil Falls. On Highway 1 in Big Sur the Mustang pulled up to a book shop owned by Rosko's old pal Henry Miller. While the two old zeitgeists sat on a redwood burl and swapped sentimental reminiscences about surrealism and Da Da in 1920s Paris, Michael

AUSTINTACIOUS: A Tale of 1968 Austin

A. bought from Mrs. Miller *Tropic of Cancer, Tropic of Capricorn* plus every other first edition in the place and a madrone roll-top desk to hold these treasures. After renting a U Haul trailer for the Mustang, Michael A. and Rosko went for a carafe of white wine and a fruit board at Nepenthe's, a restaurant on Highway 1 perched on a pinnacle overlooking the Pacific Ocean. Later, they met up with the "friends in Santa Cruz" Rosko had mentioned—Chel and Los Boys—from whose coastal freighter a ton of Acapulco gold was loaded into Red Fred's fish truck.

. . .

In Santa Clara—and in his role as Mr. Designated Spender for Xutan Partners—for $25000 of the Cacciatore cash acquired from the Petrified Forest smuggle Rosko bought 1% of NM Electronics, the startup company Taj had overheard recommended by a UT Electrical Engineering professor. Mixed in with this $25K were the Grover Cleveland $1000 bill and the William Cleveland $500 bill.

. . .

In San Francisco Li Mam took Michael A. to hear Quicksilver Messenger Service whose song "Mona" floored Michael A. Now the couple was at Li Mam's flat at Ninth and Clement near Golden Gate Park, the Small Faces' "Itchycoo Park" playing on Radio KSAN and Michael A. feeling up Li Mam, who was saying:

"If you do it just right, it'll get me really hot."

Michael A. moved his hand and said, "There?"

"More to the left."

"How's that?"

"Mmmph ... mmmm."

"We there?"

"Less talk." Sigh. "More rub."

A little heavy breathing later, Michael A. stood up in bed to beat his chest and say, "No man is an island! No man is an island!"

"From this angle he is more like a peninsula," said a much sated Li Mam.

Whereupon Michael A. plopped down beside her and said, "Do you love me, Li Mam?"

"Welll ... I don't *dis*love you."

Michael A. sighed and said, "Good thing I got a hard bark."

. . .

They stood beside an eight-inch cannon that had been an artillery piece at San Francisco's Fort Mason since before the Civil War. They were watching a Panamanian freighter with 5000 pounds of Panama Red sail under the Golden Gate Bridge. Michael A. had on his rose colored glasses, his **SECEDE** T-shirt, a pair of madras shorts and white Converse tennies. Rosko wore a white suit and Panama hat and Walks In Blue Green was clad all in buckskin.

"Who knew Nacho and Uncle Tunoose had 5000 thousand pounds of Panama Red coming this way?" Michael A. said from well behind his rose colored glasses.

"I had hell finding a parking spot for my refrigerated truck," said Walks In Blue Green.

"God bless America," Michael A. said.

"And all the ships at sea," said Rosko.

. . .

On the table was Richard Brautigan's *Watermelon Sugar*, a gift to Michael A. from Li Mam. "I like it wayyy better than *Tropic of Cancer*," she said to Michael A.'s Lebanese cousin, a U.S. Army colonel and diplomatic attaché to the Beirut embassy.

"Your daddy was a good soldier," the colonel said to Michael A. while drumming his fingers on a briefcase full of money. "I cain't say nothin finer about any man."

They were at Enrico's in San Francisco's North Beach. Across the street two of Li Mam's brothers were loading a crate marked "Household Goods" into a black van. The crate held 50 kilos of Nepalese temple ball hash shipped from the Beirut embassy to New York then to San Francisco International Airport. Because of the diplomatic immunity granted to Michael A.'s colonel cousin, there had been no inspection by U.S. customs. Behind the black van was Michael A.'s Mustang with its U Haul trailer containing Jen's olive green Samsonites and the roll-top desk holding the book shop purchases and over a half a million in cash from Red Fred and Walks In Blue Green.

. . .

A half an hour later Michael A. met up with Rosko for clam chowder at The Eagle's Nest, a longshoremen's hangout at the back end of Fisherman's Wharf.

"It was in a place such as this that I met Nacho and your Uncle Tunoose," Rosko said. "Actually Tunoose is not your uncle. You're not even related."

"Who among us is surprised?" said Michael A.

The Panamanian freighter captain who had smuggled the 5000 pounds of Panama Red then came over to their table and Rosko said to Michael A., "This is *au revoir*, mi zeitgeist. I've never been to Panama and when I arrived at 19th Street I spun your globe and my finger landed on Panama." Next he hugged Michael A., tipped his Panama hat, said "Swiss chocolate" and walked off with the freighter captain.

"Nothin' gets to you like your family," said Michael A. and got down to business with his clam chowder.

. . .

Tres said, "Mom told me that startup company Rosko bought into on behalf of Xutan Partners later became InTegral Electronics now known as Intel Corporation."

"That's right," Jack said, "and by the time Xutan Partners got out our investment had skyrocketed ten fold."

"You got out?"

"Sure. Back then Que Tal did not get it that corporations are strictly business and not 'One world. One planet!'"

"Bummer."

chapter twenty nine

When Jack learned he had passed all his courses and was off scholastic probation, he told Jen who said:

"Wonderful, dear. But late night band practices, being a momma to Baby Maya and a nurse to Natasha have landed me on scho pro."

. . .

On December 16 the Spanish government declared null and void a 1492 decree expelling Jews from Spain.

. . .

On December 17 the Federal Reserve Board raised the discount rate from 5.25% to 5.5%. Also, Nixon's Treasury Secretary designate refused to commit to maintaining the price of gold at $35 an ounce.

. . .

On December 18 major U.S. banks raised interest rates to 6.75% in an effort to halt inflation.

. . .

On December 19 Jack parked the VW bus on 10th Street in front of the three houses Xutan Partners had bought from the church ladies. Their former residences were now law offices and though each lawyer had hung out his shingle, they had used their initials instead of their first names. Jack did not know Cousin Brucie's last name, but recognizing a surname, he tried that office. Going in, it surprised him to hear Radio Reefer playing Que Tal's version of "Crossroads". Another surprise was that Two Moons was the receptionist, who showed Jack into Cousin Brucie's office saying, "I coulda stayed a Main Library page but this is on the job training."

Once they were seated, Brucie said, "First off, I'd like to express my gratitude to Que Tal for setting me up in this office."

"We need each other, Cuz, and with us it's family first ... though I don't rightly know how we're related."

"Nacho was my mother's cousin."

"Wow," Jack said, showing surprise. "I didn't know I had any other Austin cousins."

"Nobody gets to you like your family," Brucie said. Then he grinned and said, "Did Uncle Tunoose ever mention he wanted to call my law firm 'Dewey Cheatam & Howe'?"

"No. But he often said sharks don't bite lawyers as a professional courtesy."

Brucie grinned some more at this then said, "These first documents pertain only to you and Jen" and handed Jack the adoption papers for Baby Maya and another document which also made Jack smile. Brucie next handed over a sheaf of papers, saying, "These are the deeds to the 19th Street house, Castle Hostel, the church ladies' houses, the Second and a Half street house and La Vaca Lana." Giving Jack more papers, he said, "Here are the documents proving all of La Vaca Lana's business licenses' fees have been paid. Jolinda and Daphne have the actual licenses on display at the site." He then gave Jack another stack of papers and said, "These are the rental agreements for the law offices. By the way, they were smart buys since both the capitol and the university will never be moved." Next Brucie said, "Now, regarding Xutan Partners, am I correct in assuming the modus operandi is to accrue sufficient funds to live off the interest?"

"Yep."

"Where does 1174 Second and a Half fit in?"

"It'll just be Taj's workshop. He's not gonna be a NASA engineer. He's gonna be an inventor."

"That makes 1174 Second and a Half a tax write-off and"—making a note on a yellow legal pad—"it appears we'll need a patent lawyer. Now for Uncle Tunoose's will."

"He had a will?"

"He did. Xutan gets the two downtown lots and—"

"What two downtown lots?"

"The lots bought by Nacho's grandfather at the 1839 public auction to finance the State Capitol building. Cool Breeze's family has kept them profitable for nearly 150 years, first as livery stables and now as parking lots. The only time they didn't turn a profit was In World War II when they were Victory Gardens."

"Cool," Jack said, smiling. "What else is in the will?"

"Aunt Sofi gets Tunoose's cash plus 320 acres of land in east Travis County. It was Uncle Tunoose's hope that the land will remind her of the old country because he planted fig trees there in a meadow with a stream running through it. Do you think Aunt Sofi will like it?"

"She'll love it." Jack and paused to think before saying, "There's a house up on blocks at 1019 Elba Place that needs to be moved beside that stream in the meadow."

Brucie made a note of this on his yellow legal pad and said, "Tunoose also left ten leather pouches for Maya Karma Gage in a safe deposit box." Jack was wondering if those leather pouches contained diamonds when Brucie said, "Is Que Tal working New Year's Eve?"

"Nope. Unless recording in Songcatcher is work."

"The IRS will see it as such since, like Purple People Eater, Songcatcher Studio is an in-home business and therefore tax deductible." Brucie then made another note on his yellow legal pad and said, "I wonder if you and Michael A. would consider joining your two Austin cousins for a brief get-together New Year's Eve? Mrs. Medina and the rest of Que Tal is welcome too. I think all y'all will find it a novel experience. And I guarantee that the view will be spectacular."

· · ·

"*Wheee!*"

Father and daughter were playing "Horsey." Jack had placed Baby Maya astride his neck and was giving his deliriously happy child a ride around the bedroom. At the same time he was ticking off her growth progress.

"Hand to eye coordination improving. Tracks objects with eyes. Recognizes Jen an' me from across the room. Puts pacifier to mouth. We talk. We read books together."

In the meantime, Jen was making sure Maya's adoption document was centered between the James Dean and Jane Fonda posters and below the very first ever photograph of Maya Karma Gage. Once satisfied, she said, "What do you make of Nacho's grandfather buying downtown lots in Austin way back in 1839?"

"No more than I can make of that ol' ringtail tooter Nacho leaving his booty to Natasha. What's important is Maya Karma Gage's adoption is a done deal an' she's both a 'Mexican an' 'Merican citizen."

"Dual citizenship means she can own a hotel in Cancun."

"According to Cousin Brucie, we should also consider condominiums, whatever those are. But that's a ways off."

"What about that official act you and I have to perform?"

"It's in the pipeline, hon. Brucie handed me both the adoption document an' marriage license at the same time."

"That means your days're numbered, Ben Jack Gage because I already have a time, a place and a preacher."

"Well, alrighty then. Let's get 'er done."

. . .

On December 20 Johnny Winter and New Atlantis played the Vulcan. In New York City novelist John Steinbeck died.

. . .

It was December 21, the winter solstice. On this date Maya Karma Gage turned three months old and Apollo 8 began the first USA mission to orbit the moon. Across the street the Dallas Cowboys cast a pall over the Gamma Sig house by losing to the Cleveland Browns

AUSTINTACIOUS: A Tale of 1968 Austin **157**

in the NFL playoffs. A norther was forecast to arrive that night but before it did, the 19th Street kids gathered in the Crow's Nest to watch the heavens from their hamacas. They declared that it was "legendary time" and that Nacho, Uncle Tunoose and Cool Breeze were with them. Enhanced by Texas Medicine, they sat cross-legged in their hamacas and beheld a star's fall into the Underworld. In awe they watched Mother Moon journey out of the eastern horizon to enter the Big Dipper.

Taj called it "a heavenly hierophany, a colossal conviviality of events."

And all of Que Tal was sure that Nacho the daykeeper would call it "a calamity of events featuring The Forces That Are."

Meanwhile, downstairs in Jack and Jen's bedroom, Mrs. Medina held Baby Maya up to the new color TV from Oscar Snowden to see Apollo 8's perspective of Planet Earth from outer space.

"See that?" Mrs. Medina said. "We're not just the 'blue planet.' We're the *Maya blue* planet."

. . .

That same day Ryder, Two Moons and Abilene left Austin for the sovereign nation the Piegan Indians called "Where the Night Sky Is Born." They would take the train to San Antonio then the Sunset Limited to Los Angeles where they would go north on the California Flyer to Portland and, east to Glacier National Park. As they boarded, Ryder said to Taj:

"Tonight's the night, right?"

"Yes. Every hour on the hour."

. . .

Every hour on the hour that night Radio Reefer played Ryder's voice saying:

"Ye shall know the truth and the truth shall make you free. History being the best storyteller and history not having changed, be it known that on June, 1967, at 1400 hours on the fourth day of the Six Day War, without warning or provocation the *USS Liberty* was repeatedly attacked by Israeli jets in international waters off the

Gaza coast. The ordnance used were rockets, cannons and napalm. Thirty-five minutes later three Israeli torpedo boat showed up to launch five torpedoes, one of which killed 26 crewmen. In all thirty-four U.S. servicemen were killed and 173 were wounded. They claim it was a case of mistaken identity but the crew of the *Liberty* will tell you that's either a load of hooey or illicit logic or both … ye shall know the truth and the truth shall make you free."

chapter thirty

"It was a dark and yucky night" was how Que Tal described the night of the 1968 winter solstice.

For What Goes Bump In The Night the norther's arrival meant yet another fire had to be lit so he decided to cook up some of the beans he had filched from Cool Breeze's garden. He was doing this when he heard The Voice say in a commanding tone:

"Hear me, Evil, for your time to serve has come."

Next, in the mantle of pallid light in the hidey-hole, between shadow and substance, What Goes Bump In The Night beheld a rising cloud of mist. Once the cloud of mist had unfolded The Voice took form as a frail, bent figure and What Goes Bump In The Night dropped to his knees and said woefully:

"I know I been bad, that I been loud with lies an' delicious naughtiness, but please don't hurt me 'cause I'm scared to suffer."

The figure puffed up its cheeks then blew out a puff of smoke and said, "Treachery for the sake of revenge."

"Maya karma?"

"Yesss. For Natasha. Even as we speak she takes what is yours and thus she must say goodbye to the sky."

"Okay with me," What Goes Bump In The Night said. "And Maisie's gonna get it too for pulling the wool over my eyes. Yeaaah, let's make it a big finish. I'll torch the root cellar and let the whole house burn, baby, burn."

"That's crazy."

These words prompted What Goes Bump In the Night to say in a loud voice, "Crazy, crazy, crazy. Come on, crazy, light my fire." Next he looked at the ceiling above which was Maisie's bedroom and said, "'Revenge is a kind of wild justice.'" It was then that darned cat brushed by his skinny leg and, from the root cellar, he heard Jack say:

"That's a line from Francis Bacon, Taj. An' you were right about where there's smoke there's fire an' that ghosts don't light fires."

. . .

That same dark and yucky night Michael A. came home. After backing his fastback Mustang into the driveway and guiding the U Haul trailer into the garage, from the Mustang's trunk he took Jen's olive green Samsonite suitcases. He was going up the back porch steps when, from above, he heard:

"Meow."

"Hello to you too," he said to Hannah up in the Crow's Nest. Then he entered the house, went through the kitchen and in the dining room around the church-door-turned-dining room table was the rest of Que Tal—and to his considerable surprise Hannah was beside the Stromberg Carlson television set. Stunned, Michael A. said, "Hannah was just up in the Crow's Nest. How'd she get here?"

"She uses brick steps in the air shaft that's alongside the chimney," Natasha said.

"Curiouser an' curiouser," Michael A. said then set down the Samsonites and said to Jen, "Sister Woman, I'm hopin' you'll soon get your precious luggage back."

"You're finally finished with them?" Jen said.

"Clean break?" said Natasha.

"Just about," Michael A. said, showing his sly grin. "First we gotta find that cave under the house that Ryder's copper rod went into an' see if it's a big enough hidey-hole for a roll-top desk an' the three lock box."

Jack said, "I'd say our best bet is beyond the root cellar."

"I agree," Taj said.

"Now just a darn minute," Jen said. "Is this desk full of money?"

"Yep, chock full same as your Samsonites," Michael A. said. "We're rich 'uns beyond our wildest dreams and,' unless this house burns to the ground, we're set for life. Folks like us can't spend all we got in double our lifetimes." Then he said, "Now tell me how come we got this old house all to ourselves again. Where's the rest of our crash pad pals?"

"Buck'n Bubba met their goal with the Petrified Forest smuggle and are now crop-dustin' up on the Caprock," Jen said with a big smile. "Two Moons and Ryder have gone back to The Rez for the holidays and Abilene tagged along."

"Cool," Michael A. said. Then to Jack he said, "I had a good visit with Aunt Asilee."

"Glad to hear it. What all'd she allow?"

"She allowed as how she'd be right proud to use Xutan moolah to clothe street people even though she doesn't know what one is. Says she'll hire forty folks an' wants to call the business 'Empresa Lanaropa'."

Jack then told Michael A. about what was in Uncle Tunoose's will. Michael A.'s response was to show his sly grin again and say, "

"You say these downtown lots only work five days a week? How's about we start up a weekend farmer's market?"

"Right on," said Jen. "I know that Mrs. Smalley and the church ladies grow more stuff than they use."

"An' I betcha Big John'd pitch in on a flea market," Jack said.

"I am certain that Cool Breeze's folks would want to vend their food," said Taj.

This was when there came a scratching in the living room wall followed by the ring of the old timey ringer on the front door and Hannah made a beeline for the entryway. Whereupon all of Que Tal got a collective smile and Michael A. said:

"Mayhaps might I interest y'all in a home away from home? It's an underground missile silo miles from nowhere that comes with a five-year food supply, a heckuva hidey-hole annnd"—wink, wink—"it ain't haunted."

. . .

It was just after first light and Taj was in his room looking at the rising sun through the east window. By now Old Man Winter had taken every leaf from Wiley and Beep Beep's favorite oak tree, so Taj basked in the sun rays' brilliance until their warmth inspired him to wheel around and strike the pose of the Jaguar Warrior. Next he was amazed to see a rainbow on the wall shared with the dining room. Taj now looked toward the north window and saw the dreamcatcher there creating the rainbow by deflecting sunlight through the hole in its center. Knowing that the center hole had to hold a prism to do this made Taj recall that, according to Chel, the dreamcatcher came from "a woman of practical wisdom" and that good dreams were supposed to pass through that center hole to the sleeping soul. So, inspired even more, Taj said to the rainbow:

"I am another like yourself."

This was when Taj heard Hannah meow on the other side of the dining room wall. Opening the connecting door, he heard her next meow come from behind the faded red couch. Going over there, he got down on his hands and knees and saw an opened panel. This was when he heard Mrs. Medina say from her room below:

"Tiny Dancer? Mona? Rain Shadow? The Voice by the Fire?"

. . .

Bicycle Annie was once more driving Natasha and Michael A. to Mueller Municipal Airport on Manor Road and again she was driving what had been Cool Breeze's 1956 pink Cadillac. Michael A. was riding shotgun and Natasha was in the back seat. As the pink Caddy headed east on 19th Street, Michael A. turned to give Natasha a sly grin and say over the top of his rose colored glasses:

"How quaint. Once more the anarchist an' the male chauvinist pig are about to fly the friendly skies."

Natasha said, "And again I remind you I am a revolutionary, not an anarchist."

"Check," he said and reached down to slip a C-note into his white Converse tennies. "An' for this trip I am I.B. Gilligan an' I.B. is tying up loose ends."

Bicycle Annie said, "And I still maintain that both of you are bourgeois capitalists."

Now looking at Natasha again and noting that she was wearing chanclas, Michael A. said, "Eschewing our combat boots, are we?"

"I'm on furlough from the War Against Greed."

"Are you sure you're well enough to travel?"

"I'm fine. Quit worrying about me."

"You know I can't quit worryin' about you 'cause part of love is worry." Then he said, "So our resident heiress and revolutionary is returning to Where The Sky Is Born. Will she be staying in her Cozumel penthouse? Or mayhaps on her yacht as she sails to Cuba for a chat with Fidel? An' what's the latest with you'n Oily George? You hooking up him down on the island?"

"None of your bee's wax on all those questions. But as an empowered woman I will say that I got great pleasure giving Oily George the air." Next she said, "Regarding loose ends, I.B. Gilligan, I don't see Jen's olive green Samsonite suitcases or your handwoven, beaded elkskin medicine bag."

"The Samsonites are in the trunk," Annie said.

"And I've downsized from the medicine bag," Michael A. said, holding up an attaché case. "I got it at the Sears in Hancock Center for a paltry $4.44."

"Plus 4% tax," Annie said.

Michael A. said, "So what *is* the story on this Cozumel trip, Natasha? Heading down to Where The Sky Is Born for another journey of personal discovery, are ya?"

"It's to see about my inheritance," she said. Then she took out a leather pouch from her hippie purse and said, "And this."

"Whoa!" Michael A. said "More diamonds from Rosko?"

"Nope. They're Uncle Tunoose's ashes and they're going in—"

"The River of Time. Of course. I hope you see a dolphin on that dive. A dolphin is your uay, right?"

"You know it is. To la maya they are water jaguars."

Bicycle Annie said, "Do you have a uay, Michael A?"

"Yep. He's a Martian named Marvin."

"Marvin's a cartoon character," Natasha said to Annie.

"That's hardly surprising for a bourgeois dope fiend," she said.

"Who's your uay, Annie?" Michael A. said.

"Locahantas. The other Bicycle Annie."

"*La otra*. Princess of the Drag Tribe," Natasha said. "I saw her yesterday."

Michael A. said, "I know that Jack an' Jen's uays are a pair of peregrine falcons but Taj's uay is a mystery." Then he surprised Natasha by saying, "Now that you're a rich 'un are you gonna dump Que Tal?"

"Hell, no. I may even give away my inheritance."

"Why?"

"Because less is more. Because I like what we're doing and I wanta be in our band until my dying day." Sounding nice as pie as she said, "Because I love your bass playing and you're a darn good singer. And that Quicksilver song 'Mona' we did last night really rocked."

"All I can say is I'm still your smitten kitten," Michael A. said.

"I'll always love you," Natasha said. "You were my first."

"Really? I was the first?" They were approaching the terminal now and as the Caddy pulled up to the curb, Natasha said:

"Nah, I lied. I'm pulling your leg."

"But whyyy?"

"'Cause ya killed the moment."

"How'd I do that? I thought we'd clicked again."

"Me too but Mr. Dynamic Tension hadda pop off with that 'you gonna dump us' crack." Then she got out of the Caddy and, walking away, said, "Swiss chocolate."

"Hey—"scrambling after her—"Rosko said the same thing when he left for Panama. What's it mean?"

"I was hoping you knew. It was the last thing he said to me."

This was when the pink Caddy drove off with Annie waving goodbye and saying, "Y'all stay sweet now, ya heah?"

. . .

On December 23 one dead body and 82 members of the crew of *USS Pueblo* were released by North Korea.

On Christmas Eve afternoon those in the 19th Street house were hanging out in the Crow's Nest hamacas when Hannah stopped chasing a squirrel and leaped atop the red chimney to stop dead still and stare at a circular rainbow in the sky.

"Lawsy mercy," said Jack.

Jen said, "What is that over Cambridge Tower?"

"It is a sun dog," Taj said. "A sun dog is an optical phenomenon caused when sunlight passes though cirrus clouds of ice crystals to create an internal reflection."

"It makes me think of Palenque," Jen said to Jack.

"Me too," he said. "I can almost hear Nacho saying it's 'a calamity of events featuring The Forces That Are."

So they decided once again that it was "legendary time" and that Nacho, Uncle Tunoose and Cool Breeze were with them.

chapter thirty one

For her Christmas present to the 19th Street house Boo Boo laid an egg in the middle of the terra cotta statuette next to the Stromberg Carlson television set.

December 25 was a rite of passage for someone else in the house, too. But for Jen it was in triplicate. First, it was her 21st birthday; second, she had legally become an adult; and third, it was her wedding day. These heavy changes plus parenthood came home to roost when Jen was in the shower belting out Aretha Franklin's "(You Make Me Feel Like) A Natural Woman."

"Jack," she said, coming out of their bathroom in her birthday suit, "you're gonna have to cut me some slack today 'cause I'm jarred by the officiality of adulthood, marriage and being able to vote."

"I hear ya, hon."

. . .

Just before dusk, Jen and Jack went for a spin on Lake Austin in their cayuco *Analuz*. Baby Maya, swaddled in an infant-sized Mexican blanket from Aunt Asilee, went along in her bassinette. Jack wore a tuxedo and his Granpa's Lucchese boots, the ones given to the old man fifty years ago by Governor Ma Ferguson for protecting the border against Pancho Villa. Meanwhile, the bride was also a fine sight to see in a Mexican wedding dress from Hoochie Mamas and

Granma Gage's old boots. She was also pie-eyed on Senor Fuego tequila.

Jack pulled *Analuz* parallel to the Laguna Gloria shoreline then got out to pull the bow ashore so Jen could hand him Baby Maya and come ashore. The bride and groom then strode arm in arm up the path to Laguna Gloria's gazebo overlooking Lake Austin. Here they met up with Wet Willie who had walked down from Laguna Gloria's 1916 Italian style villa. Willie, also in a tuxedo and boots, carried a magnum of champagne wrapped in a white linen napkin. Noting Jen's condition, he handed her the magnum then began the wedding ceremony by saying:

"First off, let me say that you two make a beautifully handsome couple. Also, be it known that I'm a bona fide preacher in the Universal Life Church an' I got a little card to prove it."

"Just get 'er done, Willie," Jen said after a swig of bubbly.

"Do we have a witness?" Wet Willie said.

Baby Maya then gurgled, so Wet Willie said, "It appears we do." Next, after Jen swigged more champagne, he said, "We are gathered here today to—"

"I gotta pee," Jen said.

"An' Maya's a mite seasick," Jack said.

Which was when Jen took another swig of champagne then stripped the white linen napkin off the magnum and handed it to Jack. Jack spread the white line napkin on his left shoulder and was patting Maya on the back to burp her when Jen said:

"Time's a-wastin so me'n Jack'll just ad lib the vows."

"You're on," Jack said and got to it: "Jen, I vow not to bug you any more about the letter from your father."

Jen took another swig and said, "An' I'll lay off raggin' ya 'bout school."

"I vow we won't never hang in the wind again."

"Ouu, Jaaack, my head's spinnin'."

"Then quit guzzlin' the bubbly, goshdawg it."

"It is what it is an' what it is, Jack, is what it'll be."

Which was when Baby Maya burped up baby spit yellow urp on the white linen napkin on her father's shoulder and Wet Willie handed diamond rings to the bride and groom and said:

"I hereby pronounce you two man and wife."

"For as long as our love shall last," said Jen, eyes spinning like pinwheels.

"Yes, ma'am," said Jack.

"May I kiss the bride?" said Wet Willie.

"B-bride?" Jen said, and vomited all over Wet Willie.

. . .

While Aunt Sofi minded Baby Maya, Jack and Jen dined at Victor's Italian Restaurant at 29th and the Drag. Just like their last time here on Valentine's Day, they got the same candlelit table for two. Once again they ordered a bottle of Chianti, dinner salads and plates of lasagna plus a basket of garlic bread. Also like Valentine's Day, Juan—still an unappealing young man with mutton chop sideburns, dark hair parted in a hard line and slicked down with Brylcreem and wearing a long-sleeve white shirt with black bow tie and dark trousers—played something romantic on his violin. Though Juan was still awful on the violin, Jen again pretended to swoon. After Jack had tipped Juan a buck so Juan would leave, Jen, eyes on her diamond wedding ring, said:

"Jaaack?"

"Yeah, hon?" Mouth full of garlic bread.

"I don't remember our wedding. Did we do it right?"

"Oh hell yeah. It was right as rain."

"Good." Pensive before saying, "Jack, do you recall how in psychology class I learned there are three types of romantic relationships? Lust, love and companionship."

Jack took a swig of Chianti and said, "I do an' I still think we're all three an' won't ever get past the love kind of romantic relationships."

"Awww, how sweet." Then Jen gave him that certain look and said, "Will you talk Spanish to me tonight in bed?"

"Sure. Unless it disturbs our Maya."

After another pensive moment, Jen said, "What do you think Michael A.'s doing right now?"

"Oh, he's probably holed up somewhere havin' fun."

"Is '*holed* up' guy talk for 'lovin the ladies?'"

"Yep. I'd bet dollars ta donuts he's gettin' his horns shorn."

. . .

Playing on the radio was The Doors'"Love Me Two Times." Lying on the floor were her push-up bra and bikini panties next to his cutoffs and **SECEDE** T-shirt. But, unlike Graciela la cubanita, Michael A. was not entirely nekkid as a jaybird because he still had on his white Converse tennies. They were in Boca Raton, Florida, at 610 High Street, a house of ill repute run by The Lavendar Thrill Gang . They had just finished being intertwined like fornicating reptiles for the second time and Michael A., his godawful ugly toes now uncurled, was saying:

"A show like what Mugsy's talking about—freighters, yachts an' big ass speed boats—is both risky and real. Real expensive."

"Ohhh, si?" said Graciela, nuzzling him with her nose.

Michael A. grinned and said, "You know what, darlin'? I happen to be acquiring quite an affection for you."

"An' I be acquiring mucho appreciation for *tu tambien*, Marvin." Saying it "Marveen."

It was then that outside their door came a hubbub of yelling followed by—*kaboom!*—and their door was kicked in and a cop yelled "Reach for the sky, longhair!"

"Mubblefubble," said Michael A. "Not at all providential."

. . .

Scuba had just given Natasha a nickel tour of San Miguel, having driven Lurch away from the touristy part of San Miguel onto unpaved, dusty back streets past cantinas with names like El Zacil, El Alux, El Balam, simple places where Cozumel Maya sat and talked and laughed while they ate and drank beneath thatched roofs. Being a tad tipsy, Scuba had driven Lurch a bit erratically and had narrowly avoided sideswiping parked cars. Lurch fit right in on the back streets, of course, the vehicles there also having different colored fenders and bumpers, most of them a disintegrating hodgepodge of reborn and recycled taxis and rent-a-cars. Natasha was tipsy, too, but she was determined to keep a level head, not do anything she would be sorry for in the morning.

Now they were with Chel in Rick's Café Americain and Chel was suggesting they have an appetizer like *uech* or *te'pes'kin't'le*. When Natasha said she had no idea what these dishes were, Scuba said:

"They be armadillo'n guinea pig."

"Sorry, I don't eat my fellow sentient beings," said Natasha.

"Then try the *x'ni'pec* salsa," Chel said. "It's all veggie."

"No thanks. I don't eat what I can't spell either."

Richie Valens' "La Bamba" now came on the juke box and this inspired Natasha to kick off her chanclas and climb atop the table. There she hiked up her Maya blue skirt and commenced to dance with one arm swinging free while holding a leather pouch in her hand.

"The Bridge of Sighs is my favorite dreaming spot," she yelled down to Chel and Scuba. "Any Cozumel Maya diver knows the way and soon Uncle Tunoose'll be recyclin' fo'ever'n ever."

"Oblivion gets us all," said Scuba.

"You said it, brother," Natasha said. "But before it does, I wanta sail to Cancun an' see what that's about. Then I wanta cruise over to Cuba'n see an' meet up with Fidel."

"And what about your cocoa farms in Guatemala?" Chel said.

"Swiss chocolate," Natasha said, and got off the table because the waiter had brought their drinks. Seeing the waiter made Scuba uneasy, after the waiter left she asked Scuba why.

"Juan Carlos has that effect on me," he said.

"Nobody gets to you like your family," Chel said.

. . .

Natasha was Alice in Wonderland in a T-shirt that said DEEP THINKER and she was sure that being down here in The Deep was just what she needed.

A mere few minutes ago, just after twilight, the Delphinus Constellation low in the eastern sky, Natasha had rolled off the *Zak Be's* dive platform to dive down into the Octopus's Garden. After saying hi to the octopus, the sea cucumber and the granddaddy conch—*zoom!*—she had made a 200-foot beeline down here to her favorite dreaming spot. She was hovering in a full lotus inches above the Bridge of Sighs, the span of coral between two cave mouths in the cave system la maya called Xibalba. As soon as she released Tunoose's ashes into the Gulf Stream—the River of Time—an eagle ray exited Xibalba's fourth level, the cave to her left. Something told Natasha that the eagle ray was Tunoose's uay so, as it passed her on its way across Xibalba's fifth level—the Bridge of Sighs—to enter Xibalba's sixth level, the cave to the right, Natasha struck the dancing pose of the Jaguar Warrior. And this was when she heard Nacho's voice say:

"The center of of this house shall never die."

In the next moment a large shadow passed over Natasha, and this mysterious immensity caused Natasha to look up and see her uay the water jaguar, this dolphin giving her a Cheshire cat grin.

So Natasha grinned back a Cheshire cat grin of her own.

Because she was Alice and this was Wonderland.

. . .

Jen said to Michael A., "How come you missed Christmas at home?"

"I was unavoidably detained."

"It was a woman, wasn't it? Money and misery, misery and pain, right?"

"Yes an' no. Anyway, I got locked up."

"You spent Christmas in the calaboose?" Jack said.

"Only a little bit of Christmas. The C-note in I.B. Gilligan's tennis shoe bailed me out." Jen then gave Michael A. a buss on the cheek which startled him and made him say, "Criminey, Jen! What was *that* for?"

"A kiss from the bride. You looked like you needed it, you ol' booger eater."

Michael A. then turned to Jack and said, "You ratted me out?"

chapter thirty two

They were now on the western outskirts of the Dallas-Fort Worth Metroplex and Jack was saying, "When we were born there was the Five and Dime store and there were two billion people on the planet. Now it's the Family Dollar and there are six billion of the Virus That Is Us."

"They say the Austin metroplex has two million people and will be four million by the next generation," Tres said.

Jen said, "Now I ask you—is that evolution or devolution? Think about it: the Second and a Half Street property goes from a rent house for the Medinas to Taj's workshop to a laundromat then a parking garage and now it's an office building. In the meantime the two downtown lots have gone from Victory Gardens and parking lots to highrises."

Jack set aside The Big Bend Sentinel and said, "The final chore of development is dealing with old age. You lose your hair but get squiggly eyebrows'n tiny hairs creepin' outta your ears."

Jen said, "Old age is a drag, literally, because it slows your life down to a crawl."

"Hell," Jack said, "I can barely pick a guitar 'cause of my arthritis."

"And my osteoporosis is about to pop my ol' back in two," Jen said.

Jack said, "We no longer look to the future because the past is what we see on accounta it's where we wanta be. Shoot, even though my memory's practically all that's left of me, I can't answer fill-in-the-blank questions anymore, they gotta be multiple choice."

Jen said, "Would you believe that one reason I read the newspaper is to learn what day it is?"

"Geezerdom is not knowing if you'll make it to the bathroom on time," Jack said.

"Depends," Jen said, and burst out laughing.

"Well," Tres said, "at least you two are young at heart."

"Bulll, Ben Jack the Third," Jen said. "We're withered grapes an' you know it."

"Life truly is a trip," Jack said. "It's the journey from innocence to experience."

"But you don't choose a life," Jen said, "you love a life."

"I sure wish I'd seen 200 West 19th before the University gobbled it up," Tres said.

"At least we have these photos," Jen said, holding up the shoe box in her lap.

Jack said, "And thank goodness for Candid Teac."

. . .

Because Taj had wired the Teac reel to reel tape recorder to come on whenever Songcatcher Studio's light switch was flipped on, any human activity within was captured on tape. From October until the middle of December, 1968, the Teac produced a time capsule of oral history that Que Tal called "Candid Teac."

"It's where we broke through the noise an' got down with our sound," was how Michael A. put it.

Naturally, much of Candid Teac was the mundane, nonverbal noise of chairs and band equipment being moved around, instruments being tuned, microphone checks, quarts of Old Milwaukee being broken. Some of what was recorded involved Baby Maya being burped or having her diaper changed, both acts provoking someone to proclaim "Tinkle, tinkle, little star" or "Author! Author!" or "Strike a match!" Or "Let this be a lesson that condoms are easier to change than diapers." Or "Who floated the gas biscuit?" Or "Fault the finder for it lies behind her." Or "Goldurned dawgs."

There was also Natasha saying to Jen, "While sailing back from Cozumel I saw music on the water same as if it were wind" followed by Jen saying, "Right before we left the desert, I saw music on the wind. It made me realize that while harmonizing we could see ourselves in the music ." Followed by Michael A. chiding them, saying, "Hey, listen to the Zen hens." Followed by "Booger eater!" from Jen and "Sit on it'n rotate, spitbird!" from Natasha.

And then there were those genuinely cool moments like when Pearl dropped in and she and Jen did a duet of "Trouble In Mind." Not only was the song preserved on tape but so was Pearl's philosophy: "If you ain't livin' on the edge, you're takin' up too much room."

And then there were Jen's rebel yell screams.

And Jack's "Useful now is necessary later" and "I say we 86 the Throwaway Society."

And Natasha's "Electronic media of the global village is the medium that is the massage."

And Wet Willie's "I see by my outfit I'm a cowboy."

And Ryder quoting William Burroughs: "The past is fiction."

And Taj saying, "Connectivity via biomimicry is a conviviality of events that is CoEvolution and that means we are truly convesting."

And Michael A. saying, "Did you know that Cheetah the chimp is *stilll* alive?"

Plus there were Que Tal's exchanges about doing what they loved. After great takes of new songs—Natasha's "I'm Gonna Get Some,"

Jen's "Love Me Wild," Taj's "Hideous Does It" and Jack and Michael A.'s "Maya Blues"—Michael A. was heard to say, "Five part harmony will always win me over" with Jack adding, "Yeah, it's tough enough to kill you but soft enough to change you."

chapter thirty three

On the afternoon of New Year's Eve Michael A. took Jack to the Scho Pro Lounge off 29th Street. Jack got a table and Michael A. used one of the expiration-free *Daily Texan* coupons to buy a $1 pitcher of beer. Next Michael A. dropped a quarter in the juke box and then joined Jack just as "Street Fightin' Man" was starting up.

"What have you learned in 1968, Jack?"

Jack did not hesitate. "Femininity is no weakness."

"Yeah, it's brought me to my knees many a time," Michael A. said. "So how's married life?"

"Same as before only more so."

"Think you can handle it?"

"As Granpa Gage would say 'No hill for a climber.'"

"I miss that old man," said Michael A. "An' I miss Uncle Tunoose an' his 'Women are nothin' but misery an' pain.' Also his Thorsten Veblen stuff, the 'no witnesses, no crime' bit an' 'no mota with the moolah.' An' I miss Cool Breeze quoting Shakespeare. "'Tis an unweeded garden that grows to seed.'"

Jack said, "Don't forget Nacho and his 'Look to the past for lessons an' the future for answers' an' all that other 'so say la maya' stuff."

"But we've lost those wise men," Michael A. said wearily.

"An' Aunt Asilee says Scooter Culero may as well be MIA 'cause he durn sure ain't all there no more."

"Ain't life a trip?" Michael A. said. "I mean, seein' as how you'n me'n ours is sittin' pretty? Hell, we's rich'uns."

"We're also free," said Jack. "Oh hell yeah we are."

"I guess 1968 has been the best an' worst of times," Michael A. said. Then he took a sip of beer and said, "Kudos on gettin' off scho pro, Cuz."

Both stayed quiet, thoughtful until Michael A. said, "Ya know what? Cool Breeze's quote about 'grows to seed' has reminded me that Chel gave me a bunch of seeds last September. He called 'em 'Nacho's South American seeds' an' said Nacho wanted us to plant 'em."

Jack said, "I know of 320 acres good for growin' figs."

"That does seem like a good way to find out what they are." Then Michael A. said, "So, seein' as how you're a married man with a baby an' all like that, you're not interested in Mugsy's Ceebo business?"

"Sorry, Cuz. Cain't do it."

"Ya know I gotta go rogue an' step out with Mugsy, doncha?"

"I figured as much, seein' as how the outlaw life not only gets you to feel the pixie in ya, it also makes you powerfully alive."

"It sure does keep ol' Marvin the Martian wonderin' where the kaboom is," Michael A. said.

"You gotta be you," Jack said then raised his mug and said, "To success, to crime."

"I knew you could dig it," Michael A. said and they clinked mugs in solidarity. Next Michael A. said, "So how do you'n Jen like them weddin' rings Ryder made with Rosko's diamonds?"

Jack looked at his and said, "We love 'em."

"Then how would you feel about Xutan Partners backing Ryder in a jewelry store?" Then he grinned and said, "We could put it in La Vaca Lana an' call it 'Baudy Baubles.'"

"I can dig that too," Jack said, smiling. "But ya know what I could *really* dig right now, Cuz?"

"Bitin' into a six-bit steak at GM Steak House or a chicken fried steak an' fries at Hank's?"

"Hank's is closer," Jack said. Then, getting up to leave, he said, "But don't tell Jen."

. . .

For sunset Tuesday, December 31, 1968, Que Tal was in their hammocks, these hamacas now strung from the attic's rafters to the sill of the dormer window in the roof. This setup let everybody enjoy the view south through Austin's skyline dominated by the Capitol and Cambridge Tower, the latter's west side now in a violet hue from the setting sun.

"Even if it is New Year's Eve an' we got no gig, I ain't the least bit sorry," Jack said. "Not having to haul band equipment in an' outta the VW bus then in an' outta of a gig an' back to Songcatcher is plenty fine by me an' my game leg."

"That brings up a question we need to ponder," said Michael A. "When our music starts speaking to the souls of a million strangers, are we gonna just give in an' live in a fishbowl?"

"*Phooey* on being famous!" Jen said, making a face. "*Phooey* on press conferences! *Phooey* on giving autographs!"

"And if our gigs were to evolve into concerts" Taj said, "some fans will be mad if we don't play what they want to hear."

"And, hey, it's tough enough pondering the price of the wealth we've just come into via the underground economy," Natasha said. "I don't need the added hassle of dealing with a manager and record company or an entourage of hangers-on. Less *is* more."

"Y'all know I'm a shy guy," Jack said. "Fortune's fine but fame and its demands'd be a curse for this ol' country boy."

"I don't want to make the world," Michael A. said, "an' I don't want the world to make me."

Jen said, "So we just make our music in Songcatcher and let Teac preserve it?"

"Why not?" Taj said. "The Beatles have their own record company."

"They no longer tour either," said Jack. "So, yeah, let it be,"

All of Que Tal now looked each other in the eye and, one by one, they nodded at each other. Next Taj reached down and picked up a sheet of music that had been left over from when the house was The Waterloo Music Academy. After wadding it up in his hand, he began patting out a beat with his right foot then countering it with downbeats from his left foot. Next, as he had on the front porch nearly a year ago when the 19th Street kids decided to become a band, Taj started squeezing out a rhythm on his wadded-up paper accordion, one that had a marimba-like sound. Then, also like almost a year ago, Jen hummed a Cream song—"I'm So Glad" this time—and soon Que Tal was harmonizing it. When done, Bicycle Annie yelled from within the house:

"Ain't nothin' like five part harmony. Now all y'all get in here an' take a look at what the cat dragged in."

. . .

So there they were at long last: 801 Red River. It was nine o'clock, New Year's Eve. All five members of Que Tal wore generic T-shirts. Jen's said FUN FOR ALL AGES; Jack's said CLIMATE CONTROLLED; Natasha's said VOID WHERE PROHIBITED; Taj's said USE ONLY AS DIRECTED; Michael A.'s said DOES NOT COME FULLY ASSEMBLED. In front of a decades-old building made of mortared limestone blocks stood Que Tal beneath a yard arm from which was suspended a faded black wooden sign showing a silver knight below medieval lettering saying *The One Knite Dive & Tavern*. Since Texas law in 1968 forbade a view into a bar, the windows on each side of the door were blacked in. John Lee Hooker's "Hootchie Coochie Man" could be heard on the juke box inside, though.

"At long last the time has come to chat about cabbages an' kings," said Michael A.

"Also to decide if this is a circumcised idea," Jen said.

"What's the rent?" Natasha said.

"A hunnert a month," said Michael A.

Jen said, "And the lessors are getting out because?..."

"They're law students about to graduate."

Natasha said, "I don't like it that the police station is only a block away."

"The pigs don't need us," said Michael A.

"And, man, they expect the same," Jack said.

Jen now opened the door and said, "Let's get this over with."

AUSTINTACIOUS: A Tale of 1968 Austin

The entryway was an upright coffin, a City of Austin Fire Department sign on it declaring occupancy was limited to one hundred people. The One Knite was a small club, maybe fifty feet deep and twenty feet wide. To the left of the entryway was a short pinetop bar that had lots of names and initials carved into it but only half a dozen bar stools. The bartender was a hippie who answered to "Merle" and behind him, against the wall, was a reach-in beer cooler. At the far end of the bar a redheaded hippie chick was selling sandwiches. To the right of the bottomless coffin entrance and against the wall were a pair of pinball machines beside a juke box and cigarette machine. Between these machines and the bar was barely enough room for a pool table where a game of nine-ball was underway and at which a guy named "Roger" was cueing up to sink the money ball. Except for the bathrooms to the left of the stage against the back wall, funky tables and chairs took up the rest of The One Knite. The rear exit was a door at the left of the stage on which Arbor Vitae was setting up their equipment. Through this exit was a balcony that overlooked Waller Creek.

"It's ouu spooky dark in here," Natasha said.

"The One *Knite*, darlin'," Michael A. said. "One *night*."

"Perhaps as in Elvis's "One Night With You," Taj said.

"Or maybe a 'fade to black' theme," Jen said. "But, hey, check out the junk hanging from the ceiling. They got a typewriter, an adding machine and all sorts of other crap."

"Their interior decorator is probably Big John," said Jack.

"I like the hippie ambiance," Natasha said. "Note the commode at the end of the bar. It's got a mannequin's legs in black fishnet stockings standing in it and"—snickering—"the front of the commode has a bumper sticker saying "Down With Communism."

"It's a helluva dive, ain't it?" Jack said.

"Yep, what we got here is your basic den of iniquity," Michael A. said and then headed for the bar.

The rest of Que Tal took a table with rickety chairs. Around them were college students, necking couples, ageless hipsters, juiced-out juicers, hookers, off duty cab drivers and other street types.

"This is like The Cellar in Fort Worth," Jen said to Jack.

"Cool, ain't it?"

Michael A. now came back with mugs and a pitcher of Lone Star. After filling his mug, he said, "Yep, a hippie bar is just what Austin's counterculture needs."

"I know it's what I want," Jack said as he filled his mug. "I been cravin' a place where I can cut loose to my kind of music with my kind of people."

Next, Jen filled her mug, took a sip and said, "The beer's cold."

Everybody was quiet a moment, sipping on their beer and looking around The One Knite until Michael A. framed his hands like a movie director envisioning a scene and said, "I can see it now—we'll bill it as 'the joint that won't go out'."

"'The dive too tough to die'," Jack said.

"Also a dive with no cover charge," Michael A. said.

"Never a cover?" said Natasha.

"Nope," said Michael A. "We'll just pass the hat."

"I like it," Taj said then sipped his beer. "New bands can debut here and I shall acquire a second Teac in order to record every moment, musical and otherwise."

"I'll draw'n print band posters," Michael A. said.

"Radio Reefer can provide promotion," Jack said.

The band started up now, Arbor Vitae opening with "Gloria".

And Que Tal was immediately blown away.

"Wow, perfect acoustics," Michael A. said, smiling.

"That clenches it, I'm in," Jen said then took a big sip of beer.

"Me too," Natasha said. "This idea ain't circumcised, no way."

"We should broadcast all the gigs here on Radio Reefer," Taj said.

"Yeah," Jack said, "an' we'll call 'em 'Live & Local'."

"How about 'Live, Local & *Loud*'," said Jen.

"We'll stop serving alcohol on time but we'll let the bands play as long as they want," said Michael A.

"But who do we get to run the place?" said Natasha.

"How about Lightnin' an' Magoo?" said Michael A. "They're two honest hippies who ain't doin' nothin.'"

All mugs were then clinked in agreement and Taj said, "CoEvolution is connectivity via biomimicry and a conviviality of events is CoEvolution."

"What*ever*," Jen said. "We're *onnn!* Let's rock!"

. . .

Tres said, "A small intimate club with perfect acoustics and music 'til sunrise. Thanks to Candid Teac II, I got to hear legends who were just startin' out. Musicians like Jimmie Vaughn and Storm, Stevie Ray, Johnny and Edgar Winter, Commander Cody and His Lost Planet Airmen, David Bromberg and Elvin Bishop, Doug Kershaw, Billy Gibbons, Ray Benson and Asleep at the Wheel, George Thorogood, Kenneth Threadgill, The Flatlanders, Marc Pollard, Keith Ferguson, Doyle Bramhall."

"Remember the night Carol King and James Taylor and Pink Floyd dropped in?" said Jack.

Jen said, "Pink Floyd wanted to play but Jimmie Vaughn said no, 'cause it was Storm's night not theirs."

. . .

While waiting for the Tower clock to strike midnight, they stood on the site of the sniper Whitman's dastardly deed of August 1, 1966. Somehow Cousin Brucie had found a way for Que Tal and Mrs. Smalley to come up here to the observation deck via the tunnel from Littlefield Fountain, the same route used by the two cops who took out the sniper. Now, with everyone comfortably numb from Dixie cups of Mrs. Smalley's homemade peach brandy and a north wind taking the Purple Crab kite up, up and away over University Avenue, a slightly snockered Mrs. Smalley was saying:

"Hear ye, hear ye, friends'n family. In 1934 the original main building of the University of Texas was razed and construction on the Tower was begun. The actual idea for the University itself began in the Mexican Constitution of 1827 with a provision for a state university for Coahuila and Texas. The Tower's site—called "College Hill"—was acquired on January 26, 1839, and the University opened September 15, 1883." Then she pointed at the clock tower and said, "According to historian J. Frank Dobie, the clock tower made Texas's premier institution of higher learning look like it had a Greek outhouse atop it."

"Absurd juxtaposition," Jen said then took a sip from her Dixie cup and whispered to Jack, "Just how do Cousin Brucie and Mrs. Smalley know each other anyway?"

"Cousin Brucie is Cousin Mona's son."

"Mona?" No longer whispering. "As in Mona the haint?"

Hearing this, Mrs. Smalley said, "I ain't no haint."

"She didn't mean you," Natasha said. "Mona is a ghost in our house."

Michael A. said, "'Mona Devine to be precise."

"Fiddledee dee'n fiddle sticks!" said Mrs. Smalley. "What jibber jabber! What poopycock! Land sakes alive, y'all—*I'm* Mona Devine."

Brucie smiled and said, "Mother was born and raised in your house but she doesn't haunt it."

"Though one day I just might," said Mrs. Smalley with a wink. "200 West 19th has a century's worth of my family's memories starting with when Granpa got it from Yucatan."

"Whoa!" said Natasha. "Yucatan owned our house?"

"Indeed it did," Brucie said. "Texas and Yucatan became allies after seceding from Mexico because Mexico vowed to reclaim them. Consequently, in 1842 your house was built to be the Yucatan Embassy."

Jen said, "I bet that explains what the cat dragged in."

Taj said to Mrs. Smalley, "Would one of your memories be a White Mountain ice cream maker?"

"Yes, indeedy." Winking again. "Granpa bought it brand new." Then, sounding wistful, she said, "My mother died there. I was named after her. I was born an' raised an' married there. Brucie was born there. And somewhere in that house is a flag they gave us after Daddy got killed in World War I."

"That's probably the flag we hung next to my dad's flag," Michael A. said. "We'll return it as soon as possible."

Mrs. Smalley now sighed and said, "It was just too much house for Brucie'n me. So I sold it to Cousin Nacho after World War II."

"He'd always loved the place," Brucie said, "and when he found the love of his life it was their dream to raise their daughter there. But they became separated after the war and she died."

Mrs. Smalley said, "The house has always been in Nacho's and my family 'cause our grandparents were part of the Yucatecan delegation. Great Grandpa oversaw the embassy's construction."

Brucie said, "But Great Granma was a woman of practical wisdom and she made the house unique."

"How so?" said Taj.

"Since there was considerable concern about another Mexican invasion," Brucie said, "she conceived a pair of escape routes within the house that led to a cave below."

"A cave!" said Michael A. "Hidey-hooo!"

"The Indians called the cave 'Dos Ojos' because its dual entrances resembled a pair of eyes," Brucie said. "Each of the house's escape routes led down into one of the eyes. The routes were vertical shafts hidden adjacent to the fireplaces. There were two on each floor, two in the root cellar and a seventh and eighth fireplace on the floor of the cave."

Taj said, "Why were the bottom four fireplaces built?"

"For air-conditioning," said Brucie.

"A.C. in the 1840s?" Jack said. "How'd that work?"

"A chamber was built between the bottom two fireplaces that opened into the cave and this allowed the cave's cool air to waft up through Dos Ojos and into the shafts. In hot weather both chimneys were covered and this let the cooler air of the cave flow up the shafts and out into the house through the fireplaces. In later years, when the house was plumbed for gas, the four lower fireplaces were left alone but gas pipes were placed in the shafts adjacent to the four upper fireplaces. For safety, the living room fireplace was covered over, the bedroom fireplaces became closets and the dining room fireplace was hidden in the floor-to-ceiling bookcase."

"Weird," said Jack.

"It's gets weirder," Brucie said. "You see, Dos Ojos was an Indian burial ground."

Michael A. said, "A subterranean cemetery like in Paris and Rome? So the legend's true? Austin has catacombs?"

"Ouu, spooky," said Natasha.

"Let's just keep it weird and only weird," said Michael A.

Brucie said, "It should come as no surprise that Nacho saw Maya mythology in the shafts and fireplaces."

"I see it too," Natasha said. "To our Cozumel Maya daykeeper Nacho it was a system of spirit tubes, physical paths for those in the underworld to communicate with the World of Nature. And it was nine levels: four levels down from the chimney by the Crow's Nest with a fifth level across the chamber in the cave then four levels up to the top of the second chimney."

"And therefore shaped like an inverted pyramid, bottom half of the Maya universe," said Taj.

"Xibalba in Austin," said Natasha.

"And the whole deal lets much of what's said in the house be heard," said Michael A.

"Also how Hannah got around the house," said Taj.

"Who's Hannah?" said Mrs. Smalley.

"My uay," said Taj

"Mine's a goat," said Mrs. Smalley. "Anyway, the addition of running water made a back porch and it hid the root cellar. Later, the bottom two fireplaces were walled off to keep a curious scamp name of Brucie out of the cave."

"I still got in," Brucie said, grinning.

"Ryder found the root cellar," Jack said.

"And he was also wise to the cave below," said Michael A.

"I found this really cool box down there," Brucie said.

"The three lock box?" said Taj. "I found it in the attic."

"And in it," Jen said to Mrs. Smalley, "were the letters your lover wrote you in World War I."

"Well, I'll swan. Me'n Abe weren't lovers though, just pen pals, Ye gods, I was only twelve years old … never mentioned that in my letters though."

Brucie said, "Have any of you ever seen the ghost?"

Jack said, "We saw her atop a chimney."

"Actually," Taj said, "that was chimney smoke."

"She sang'n scratched inside the walls," Michael A. said.

Taj said, "I am reasonably sure that the scratching was either Hannah, Boo Boo or squirrels."

Jen said, "What about the bell we keep hearing?"

"Oh," Taj said a bit reluctantly. "Well, Jen, Ryder says that is caused by a mouse residing in the front door's old timey ringer."

"Jaaack, that's right by our bedroom."

"I'm on it, hon."

Brucie now said to his mother, "Do you think this 'ghost' might be the guy Tunoose evicted?"

"The shirttail relative?" said Michael A.

"It could be him, yeah," said Mrs. Smalley. "That no-count-neer-do-well knew about the shafts and such vengeful treachery would be just like that creep."

Jack said, "During the last norther me'n Taj went down to the root cellar 'cause we smelled smoke and when we got down there we heard somebody talking."

Mrs. Smalley said, "Betcha the smoke was from one of the fireplaces down there and he was using it to keep warm."

Taj said, "Does that mean Mona was a hoax?"

"No way," Jen said.

"*Some*thing sang 'I Know You Rider' to me," Michael A. said. He then looked at Mrs. Smalley and said, "Did you say your mom was also named Mona Devine?"

"Yes. She died in her big brass bed."

"Which bedroom?"

"The lower one on the south side."

"Ma's room," said Michael A.

"Mrs. Smalley's mother was The Voice by the Fire?" said Taj.

Natasha, who had been silent for a while, now said to Mrs. Smalley, "Where did the love of Nacho's life die?"

"In Lebanon. Nacho did business there."

"He also did business in Mexico, Spain and Portugal," Brucie said. "Somehow, he, Tunoose and Rosko profited from Mexico and Portugal being neutral and because Spain was neutralized by civil war. Lebanon was lawless so they made it their headquarters."

"'Diamonds from the African mines'," said Michael A.

"Diamonds, huh?" said Mrs. Smalley. "Nacho bought your house from me with a leather pouch full of them sparklers."

"Whenever Rosko needs money," said Michael A., "he goes into a jewelry store an' comes out with cash."

Natasha now said, "How did Nacho's lover die?"

"Cholera," said Mrs. Smalley. "In a refugee camp."

"Your tree now has roots," Taj said to Natasha. "No more Eno Onmai."

It was then that the clock tower's bell began to toll its dozen peals thus prompting Michael A. to say as man-made streaks of lighting shot through Austin's sky:

"And that's the way it is. New Year's Eve, 1968."

. . .

Off Fort Worth's White Settlement Road they drove into Greenwood Cemetery and over to the headstones of Jen's parents so she could kneel down and a capella "Swing Low, Sweet Chariot". As she did so, Michael A. told Taj, "I've said it before but I'll say it again: that girl can sing."

. . .

A few minutes later, while Johnny Cash sang Tom Petty and the Heartbreakers' "I Won't Back Down", Tres was preserving the moment, having a last look around the Tajmobile at some of Que Tal's souvenirs: the terracotta statuette with six human figurines, Rosko's scribble doodles, and, written

AUSTINTACIOUS: A Tale of 1968 Austin

on the ceiling, "Kilroy was here HUBBA HUBBA". Tres knew why Taj's prosthetic arm sported a Yippie Medic armband and why a plastic Jesus was affixed to the dashboard. He could not resist smiling at the bald spot on Michael A.'s head, and he also knew about what hung above the windshield, that it was nearly two centuries old and was "what the cat dragged in": the Republic of Texas's first flag, the Zavala flag. Furthermore, Tres was pretty sure that a photo on the wall was taken at The Fig Farm and showed what Nacho's South American seeds had wrought: stevia, a natural sweetner with no calories.

. . .

When Tres felt the Tajmobile slow down, he looked through the windshield to see they were on an Interstate 30 off ramp marked "Carswell Prison". After making one turn then another and stopping at a checkpoint, Michael A. walked down the Tajmobile's companionway, put his cell phone away and said, "We're good to go soon as Nurse Abilene and Lawyer Two Moons bring her out."

. . .

Fifteen minutes later, as the Tajmobile pulled away from Carswell Prison, Tres saw its personalized license tags: **Repotaj** *and thought that, like the Zak Be, the Tajmobile was a honey from stem to stern: a state of the art vehicle that was Maya blue in color and had a peace sign on the front and hands on its headlights to make it look like a monster in your rearview mirror. Its bumper stickers said: The One Knite Dive & Tavern, La Vaca Lana, the New Orleans Club, The Jade Room, The Hungry Horse; The Vulcan Gas Company; Oat Willie's: Onward thru the Fog; I dance country at The Broken Spoke; QUESTION AUTHORITY!; Impeach Nixon!; Caca pasa, chachalaca; We have met the virus and it is us; Que Tal, y'all!; One planet one world!; SECEDE; One world one planet!*

As a reunited Que Tal headed down The Road singing "I Feel Free", Tres sidled up next to Maya Karma Gage and said, "And the band played on."

"And they'll always will play on though they know full well that nothing lasts forever," said Maya Karma Gage. Then she took a bite of a Xutan Chocolate and said, "What exactly does the Tajmobile run on anyway?"

"Wind, solar and wave power."

"That plus Taj. Pure D Taj."

"Who's the fat old man with them, Mom?"

"Judge Kilroy."

"Judge?"

"Also retired C.I.A. To this day he still greases Que Tal's wheels."

"I honestly believe Que Tal is the real Republic of Tajmania," Tres said. "They're like a sovereign nation unto themselves."

"Yep, Que Tal is what the great State of Texas once was."

"What's that, Mom?"

"An ostentatious but gracious state of mind."

"Unfortunately, the River of Time is what's next for Natasha. The cancer's wasted her away to nearly nothing."

"Nothing but heart. Did they say where they're headed and what they're going to do?"

"They're going back to the beginning and start again 'cause that's what you do when you get to the end."

THE END

disiderata considerata

Some distant eve, somewhere, someplace, sometime ago
We came upon a place we did not know
Where in the mirror Death was not a Constant Companion,
Nor was Life the Road Home
Though I knew you and you knew me,
No one else knew and no one else would we be
In that somewhere, someplace, sometime ago
There was Walks in Beauty and Like the Nite
There was Dawn Song and Bridge Beyond the Light,
There was Marvin and Ma and Rosko,
There was Tunoose, Cool Breeze and Dancing Lightning
So intertwined were we for this Turn in Time
That somewhere here now still do we see
That somewhere, someplace, sometime ago

www.ingramcontent.com/pod-product-compliance
Lightning Source LLC
LaVergne TN
LVHW051555070426
835507LV00021B/2596